Counselling: Approaches and Issues in Education

Counselling: Approaches and Issues in Education

Helen Cowie and Andrea Pecherek

David Fulton Publishers
London

David Fulton Publishers Ltd
Ormond House, 26-27 Boswell St, London WC1N 3JD

First published in Great Britain by
David Fulton Publishers 1994
Reprinted 1997

British Library Cataloguing in Publication Data

A catalogue record for this book is available from the British Library

ISBN 1–85346–293–4

Typeset by Action Typesetting Limited, Gloucester
Printed in Great Britain by Antony Rowe Ltd, Chippenham, Wiltshire

Contents

Preface

This book aims to offer counsellors working in educational settings and teachers with pastoral care responsibilities the knowledge and understanding to support effective counselling. By encouraging a reflective stance on the counselling process, the authors seek to increase the reader's capacity to think critically about relationships and to develop appropriate skills for working sensitively and imaginatively with their clients.

The following chapters focus on: the nature of the counselling relationship; issues in pastoral care in education; two contrasting approaches to counselling; ethical issues in counselling; the process of enhancing children's self-esteem; tackling the abuse of power; dealing with the loss and grief in children; an overview of the authors' contrasting models of counselling. The authors indicate ways in which they have been able to integrate ideas and practice in this field. Although the authors consider counselling in educational setting from two theoretical perspectives – attachment theory and R.E.T. – they demonstrate how it is possible to integrate ideas and practices from both while still retaining each model's distinctive nature. By remaining open to new ideas, they argue, the counsellor can develop deeper insights into the nature of the difficulties which young people experience in their lives and so become more able to offer help and support.

Helen Cowie and Andrea Pecherek,
Sheffield, April 1994.

CHAPTER ONE:

What is Counselling?

The counselling framework

We all engage in helping relationships – either as giver or recipient. Normally we call this friendship. Consider the following dialogue which takes place one evening in a pub between a new teacher and her friend:

Teacher:	'My head of department doesn't like me. I've had an awful day.'
Friend:	'Why, what's happened?'
Teacher:	'She came into my class and told the children to make less noise. I was humiliated. They were doing group work. I was furious. She doesn't understand my methods and what I'm aiming to do. She looks at me as if I'm dirt. I can't do anything because she's my boss. The kids know. They know I'm not in charge. She completely undermines me. What shall I do tomorrow?'
Friend:	'God, how awful! I had a boss like that. I left.'
Teacher:	'I can't leave. It's my first year.'
Friend:	'You did really well on teaching practice. You were really good at it. Silly old bat. She's got a nerve. Come on, have another drink.'
Teacher:	'I can't. I've got to prepare for tomorrow.'
Friend:	'You prepared for tomorrow all weekend. You know what you're doing. If I had kids I'd want them to be taught by you. Come on, have a drink.'
Teacher:	'Oh all right. I feel better talking to you.' (They laugh together and order another round of drinks.)

For the time being, the young teacher's stress is relieved. Her friend's sympathetic listening has given her the support which will certainly help her through the evening and may even boost her confidence when she returns to work the next day. The value of friendship in alleviating personal distress should not be underestimated. Even though it is difficult to make precise measurement of the extent to which the positive outcome of 'feeling better' is the direct result of friendly support, it is well documented that people who have a friendship network are likely to benefit at times in their lives when they are under pressure. What qualities has the friend offered?

- she has been a sympathetic listener;
- she has shown that she cares for her friend;
- she has given some advice (albeit not helpful in this case);
- she has reinforced her self-image as a competent teacher;
- she has offered a temporary solution;
- she has distracted her from the problem.

Often, this is all that is needed. By sharing her problem with a sympathetic friend, the teacher reports that she feels better. She may find that her belief in herself has been enhanced. At the very least, she knows that she has a friend who accepts her as she is. However, as O'Connor (1992) points out, friendships are not always helpful to people in distress. Even an intimate relationship with a friend can in some circumstances make the person with the difficulty feel worse, for example, through feelings of increased helplessness or dependency. There may be short-term relief, but the friend's response may not solve the underlying problem. The friend in our example, over a period of time, may become tired of always listening to the same problem. She may feel that her advice is ignored or that she herself cannot see any way out of the situation. In this case, friendship may not be enough.

Let us suppose that six months later the teacher is still experiencing difficulties with her head of department. She starts to take time off school; the children become increasingly unruly; she talks more seriously about giving up teaching. The friend continues to offer support, but at times grows impatient that her advice is not taken. The problem remains.

Recently she has been crying in the staffroom at breaktime. So let us further suppose that the pastoral deputy head with responsibility for new teachers or staff welfare seeks out our teacher after school one day and invites her into the office for a cup of coffee.

Deputy: 'You don't seem at all happy this term. Is there anything you would like to talk about?'

Teacher: 'I wouldn't know where to start. I've always wanted to be a teacher and now I seem to be failing at it. I don't know what to do. I'm thinking of giving it up. My friend works in a bank, I thought I might look into that for a career.'

Deputy: 'That would be a shame as you're obviously so keen on teaching. What makes you think you're a failure?'

Teacher: 'It's Mrs Smith – my head of department. She criticises everything I do. She makes me feel as if I don't know what I'm doing. She's behind me all the time, checking up on my marking, looking at my lesson notes. She even comes into the classroom. The children know she doesn't trust me. I used to get on really well with them but now I'm looking over my shoulder all the time and I can't concentrate on the teaching. The kids are getting out of hand and I don't know how to control them. She's my head of department and there's nothing I can do.'

Deputy: 'We can look at that in a bit, but first, tell me, why is Mrs Smith's opinion of you so important? She doesn't, as you know, have ultimate authority over you and it doesn't sound as if she's been openly hostile.'

Teacher: 'Oh, I don't know. She just reminds me of my mother, never trusting me to do anything right. It's awful.'

Deputy: 'Mrs Smith reminds you of your mother and that feels awful.'

Teacher: 'At home I was always made to feel stupid. Not like my older sister who sailed through everything. My mother said I'd never get to university or become a teacher because I'm too disorganised. But when I did my teaching practice I didn't feel disorganised – for the first time in my life! But now that I'm here, in this job, with Mrs Smith behind me all the time it feels as if I'm back at home and I can't do anything right.'

Deputy: 'So you proved to yourself that you're a competent teacher but now you feel as if you're losing that confidence.'

Teacher: 'Yes, and I'm so miserable.'

Deputy: 'I can see that and that's not good.'

Like the teacher's friend, the deputy head is offering support and she is genuine in her desire to help. But the strategy she adopts is a counselling approach. You notice that the deputy head says very little though it is clear that she is listening intently. She uses some specific counselling skills which enable the teacher to explore the issue rather than avoid it. She reflects back what the teacher says in a calm, non-judgemental way; throughout, she demonstrates that she is able to feel empathy for the teacher.

A few sessions of this kind of intervention help the probationer to identify her problem, boost her self-confidence and support her in planning changes in her attitudes towards others and in her day-to-day management of her class. The teacher experiences relief that someone understands her feelings and does not judge them negatively. There is also an opportunity to check out the accuracy of her perceptions of disapproval on the part of the head of department and rejection by the pupils. She experiences empowerment as she experiments with new strategies for relating to colleagues and pupils. Her confidence increases as she finds that her fears and anxieties are normal for a newly-qualified teacher, and that they can be worked through and overcome. Through this supportive, accepting relationship, she begins to behave more positively and less defensively towards others, in particular towards others in authority.

It could happen that the intervention was not successful. Remember that the teacher's head of department reminded her of her mother. If this reaction persisted it might indicate that she remained preoccupied with unfinished business from the past. At this point it might be appropriate for the deputy head to recommend that she seeks counselling outside of the school setting, for example from a psychologist, psychiatrist or social worker.

The limits of counselling

When a child or a young person comes to a teacher for help, the teacher can advise, give information and practical help, or suggest counselling: counselling is only one of a range of facilities which could be offered. If we consider the case of a 13-year-old girl who tells her form tutor that she thinks she is pregnant, counselling may not be the first, or the most appropriate approach. She may have more immediate needs: for advice about how or when to tell her parents; for information about her body and the options available to her; for suggestions about whom to go to for practical medical or legal help. The tutor may also feel it appropriate to suggest that she would benefit from counselling, in order to help her to come to terms with what pregnancy means to her as a person, in addition to the myriad of practical considerations.

We feel it is particularly important to be clear about the nature of help which is being offered. Unlike a conversation between friends, a counselling relationship is structured in terms of time and place; there is some form of contractual relationship; and the counsellor will make systematic use of a set of skills. In school settings, an awareness of the need for a counselling approach to relationships can take a number of forms. Teachers who understand the value of close relationships will be observant of the quality of friendships among the pupils; they will notice the extent to which pupils support one another; they will create contexts where cooperative learning can take place. These teachers will be concerned to facilitate informal support networks; they will ensure that there are good relationships within the class; they are likely to be alert to children who seem to have no friends; they will notice when a child's work suddenly deteriorates; they will be on the alert when they observe uncharacteristic behaviour patterns in particular children. Once they have learned a range of counselling skills and strategies they will be in a stronger position to be actively engaged in a helping relationship with pupils at a point of crisis, for example when a child is bereaved. Where necessary and appropriate, they will then be in a position to offer counselling on a longer-term basis.

The effective counsellor

Some people are more comfortable acting in a counselling and supporting capacity than are others. Not all teachers are good counsellors and not all want to be. It is important in this field, as it is in many others, to be able to acknowledge our own limitations. This will ensure that:

- the person in need is provided with the most appropriate help
- the helper is protected from becoming involved with a helping process which is beyond their ability to cope
- there are good and frequent contacts between those involved in the helping process. (Murgatroyd, 1985, p. 11)

This book is for, and about, those teachers who want to clarify their thinking about the counselling process and how they perform and function as counsellors.

We all carry around our own individualistic views of the world based on our own experiences, our up-bringing, our beliefs. This affects not only our world-view, but the way we communicate our individuality to others and the way we interpret theirs.

People who work with other people – and that means all of us – come to establish a coherent view of what relationships are about, and this will influence the ways in which they offer support to others. For example, if a friend tells you that she is thinking of leaving her husband, your response to this information will be coloured by your own opinions of marriage; your opinion of your friend and her spouse; your moral convictions; and a host of other factors. Your way of supporting and helping your friend will reflect these beliefs. They are part of your psychological make-up.

The counselling relationship incorporates the psychological make-up of two different people. Whilst there are some fundamental techniques used by all – or certainly most counsellors – each relationship will be different.

The nature of counselling theories

Theories of counselling also reflect the differing nature of these relationships and the basic philosophical stance of the counsellor. The secret of being comfortable with your counselling style and counselling relationship is to acknowledge that different philosophies exist and are valid and to select the one or ones which fit most neatly with your own world-view.

In the past 25 years there has been a proliferation in counselling approaches. One estimate put the total at more than 400 (Karasu, 1986). Each one of these approaches claims to have a unique solution to client problems. The increase in methods has led some therapists to attempt to integrate approaches and to search for commonalities which are responsible for therapeutic success. So far it has been impossible to say precisely what it is that facilitates change in the client but some common features are beginning to emerge. In one study (Saltzman and Norcross, 1990) counsellors representing a range of theoretical orientations specified areas of agreement and disagreement in terms of clinical practice and hypotheses about the nature of the client problem. The areas which received the highest consensus were **the therapeutic relationship** and a concern for **the process of change.** Specific techniques and global theory were the areas where there was the most disagreement. Norcross (in Dryden,

1991) sees the move towards integration as necessary because it is 'a departure from the "dogma eats dogma" atmosphere that has characterised psychotherapy for decades'. By working towards consensus rather than battling for supremacy, counsellors can learn from one another and so elicit the best features of each school of therapy.

Let us look at the elements which, in our view, appear in all counselling approaches.

The counselling relationship

This is common to all approaches though some place more emphasis on it than others. Rogers (1951, 1967) stressed the core relationship between client and counsellor when he identified four attitudes on the part of the counsellor which were essential if change in the client was to occur:

> accurate empathy;
> congruence;
> unconditional positive regard;
> non-possessive warmth.

He claimed that it was the client/counsellor relationship itself which enabled change to take place.

Counsellors working in the psychodynamic tradition emphasise the centrality of the therapeutic relationship. The core elements in this relationship are:

> working through the relationship;
> acknowledging the power of unconscious processes.

Through the relationship, client and counsellor collaborate to understand the client's problems.

Counsellors working in the cognitive behaviourist traditions have not typically emphasised the relationship but rather focussed on changing the client's behaviour. However, recent formulations of this approach acknowledge its importance in enabling behavioural change to take place. Rational emotive therapists, for example, actively use Rogers' core conditions, especially unconditional positive regard and genuineness.

they view the relationship as equal and as one where client and counsellor sit down together to solve a problem.

The counselling contract

All counselling approaches contain some kind of agreement between counsellor and client that there will be a structure to the counselling. The most common aspects to this contract are:

PRACTICAL ISSUES – where to meet, for how long, how often. The client needs to know what the limits to helping are and whether he or she can contact the counsellor outside the agreed times should this be necessary. The client also needs to know how long a session is to be, how many sessions there are likely to be and when the counselling arrangement is to end. Time boundaries are especially important. Statements like 'I'm always in the staffroom whenever you need help' or 'call me anytime' can build up unrealistic expectations of the nature of counselling and may actually get in the way of helping. These are practical and logistical issues but it is very important that they are clarified at the beginning.

ETHICAL ISSUES – whether notes are taken; what goes on the file; the limits of confidentiality; responsibilities; boundaries. These issues are especially pertinent when working with children. Clients have the right to expect that their counsellor will behave in an ethical manner. It is unfortunate that some counsellors abuse this trust and that it is necessary for clear professional guidelines to be made explicit. We explore these crucial aspects of the counselling contract in chapter five.

PROCESS ISSUES – the roles of client and counsellor; the purpose of counselling; the goals of counselling; strategies which the counsellor will use. It is important that clients and counsellors have realistic expectations about the counselling process and that they are clear about the nature of counselling. It is not, for example, advice-giving or befriending, as we have said before, although these are useful forms of helping. It is important that the counsellor explains the style of counselling that they use and checks with the client that this is perceived to be an approach which is helpful. It is also important to clarify roles. For example, a client may not feel comfortable about working with a male counsellor because of previous experiences of being bullied by men. Similarly, the counsellor may have difficulties with certain aspects of the role. One inexperienced male counsellor abruptly terminated an interview with a woman because she wanted to talk about her sex life – he thought she needed a female counsellor to discuss this. As a result, the client was left feeling confused and hurt by this experience of rejection. If these issues are not dealt with early on in the counselling relationship, there is a greater chance that the counselling will be terminated early.

Working with the emotions

Most counselling approaches focus on feelings and, though the emphasis may vary, operate on the principle that, by arousing the client's emotions, change is more likely to occur. Changes in the client's mood during the session often form the basis for gaining access to important issues or for enabling the client to recapture disturbing experiences and to work through them in the safety of the counselling session.

Feelings which have been frozen because of their distressing nature can be explored. Counsellors working psychodynamically will, for example, encourage the client to bring repressed feelings into conscious awareness or reawaken difficult feelings around the early relationships with primary caregivers. Rational emotive therapists will train their clients to become more aware of automatic thoughts and encourage them to self-talk themselves through strong emotional arousal. Whatever the theoretical orientation of the counsellor, it is likely that there will be a belief in the power of the client's emotions to facilitate insight into problems leading to change through this increased understanding.

Skills

A commitment to helping children and young people towards personal growth is not sufficient. Neither is being a good, kind person. Skills are needed in order to engage in effective counselling. In our example of the troubled teacher, the main difference between the deputy head teacher and the friend is the level of *skill*. The deputy head is not behaving like a friend, and she would be failing in her aim if she were. Similarly, the friend was not behaving like a skilled counsellor. It would have been a dreary night out for the teacher to have her friend reflecting back her feelings and concerns!

Counselling skills need to be acquired and learned, and once learned need to be supervised. Supervision and training help to consolidate skills and approaches being practised. In addition to specific skills we also need to acknowledge that we all have different personal styles.

It is possible to change your style if you feel that another would be more effective.

The most important personal factor for the successful counsellor is *genuineness*. We will be referring to this throughout.

Interpretation

Whatever the theoretical stance of the counsellor, at some point the client will be presented with some form of hypothesis about the nature of the problem. Again, there are wide variations in the explicitness with which this will be done. Rogers, for example, was reluctant to impose interpretations on the client and preferred to create conditions in which clients would themselves formulate the solution to their problems. However, practitioners working in this client-centred tradition are still likely to find themselves presenting their clients with tentative hypotheses about the nature of the difficulty. The counsellor will make statements like:

> 'It sounds as if you are feeling very angry that your father never writes to you.'
> 'I know that it is hard for you to do this but I wonder if there is something that you would like to say to your mother ...'

Counsellors working in the psychodynamic tradition have typically engaged in interpretation and, though they may vary in the ways in which they communicate their hypotheses to the client, are likely to be creating the conditions of trust in the relationship which will enable the client to bring unconscious conflicts and repressed emotions into conscious awareness. The counsellor's interpretation will be presented to the client at an appropriate moment when, in the view of the counsellor, the client is ready to work with this new perspective on the problem. For example, Speltz (1990), using concepts drawn from attachment theory, is quite explicit about his interpretation of the difficulties being experienced by one mother, Judy, in her relationship with her 4-year-old daughter, Lisa, whom she found extremely difficult to manage. Yet it was also clear that Judy found it almost impossible to give the kind of care which was sensitive and responsive to the little girl's needs. In the course of counselling, it emerged that Judy's mother had been very cold and rejecting of her as a child.

> At a point where Judy was able to identify her own feelings of being 'a

> bad parent', the counsellor enabled her to reflect on her own experiences of being parented as a child and to put her in touch with unresolved conflicts from the past. At one point in the discussion Judy said, 'You know, I'm letting my mother parent Lisa through me.' By exploring this insight, she was able to develop a sense of appropriate boundaries between the relationships across two generations. The interpretation existed in the therapist's mind before it had emerged in Judy's conscious awareness and she came to an understanding of the issue through the process of counselling. (p. 420)

On the other hand, the following example, taken from Dryden (1990) gives a different type of interpretation which is, in many ways, more directive. In this situation the client wants to discuss a specific problem – giving a presentation to his peers – but in the course of this brief interview it becomes clear that the original issue has more than one dimension:

Counsellor: 'What is it about giving the presentation that you are anxious about?'
Client: 'Well, I may not do a very good job.'
Counsellor: 'Let's assume for the moment that you don't. What's anxiety-provoking in your mind about that?'
Client: 'Well, if I don't do a good job in class then my teacher will give me a poor "grade".'
Counsellor: 'Let's assume that as well. What would you be anxious about there?'
Client: 'That I might flunk the course.'
Counsellor: 'And if you did?'
Client: 'Oh, my God, I couldn't face my father!'
Counsellor: 'So, if you told your father that you had failed what would be anxiety-provoking about that in your mind?'
Client: 'I can just see my father now, he would be devastated.'
Counsellor: 'And how would you feel if that happened?'
Client: 'Oh, my God, that would be terrible, I really couldn't stand to see my father cry, I'd feel so sorry for him.'

The rationale of this book

In this book we take an integrationist stance and look for commonalities in helping processes. We believe that the proliferation of counselling theories is a positive state of affairs and reflects the complexity of human thought, feelings and behaviour.

Particularly influential to us have been attachment theory, rooted in the psychodynamic tradition, and R.E.T., rooted in the cognitive-behavioural tradition. In chapters three and four we present the essential components of each approach, illustrating its practical applications by looking at real case studies. As we worked together we became increasingly aware of commonalities despite the distinctive nature of each approach. We quote from Egan (1986):

> An effective eclecticism must be more than a random borrowing of ideas and techniques from here and there. Helpers need a conceptual framework that enables them to borrow ideas, methods, and techniques systematically from all theories, schools and approaches and integrate them into their own theory and practice of helping. (p. 9)

Beginners in counselling often have difficulty with this: they lack the confidence to find their own 'voice' in the counselling relationship. They need sympathetic help from more experienced workers. The aim of this book is, therefore, to provide trainee counsellors, and teachers with responsibility or commitment to pastoral care, the knowledge and skills needed to support effective counselling. An overriding aim is to integrate personal development with a reflective stance on issues and ideas on counselling in educational settings.

CHAPTER TWO:

Pastoral Care in School

The importance of pastoral care

Schools exist to facilitate the education of young people. Throughout history, the function of education has been seen as not only imparting knowledge, but also as helping students to learn about themselves. Self-growth and self-knowledge are integral aspects of the education system. However, schools today have entered the market economy. They have to sell themselves. One way in which they do this is through the issuing of a school booklet for prospective parents which sets out the aims and objectives of the school. These aims are described not only in academic terms, but also in terms of their social ethos. The pastoral system is the linchpin in establishing the ethos of the school. The following is a representative example taken from a 1994 secondary school handbook for parents:

> We aim to create opportunities for young people
> (i) to develop their abilities positively through curricular and extra-curricular activities;
> (ii) to grow in awareness of and responsibility for themselves and others;
> (iii) to understand and contribute to the ever-changing multicultural community that is both the school and society in general.
> We aim to encourage our young people to make full use of these opportunities and to provide an educative, caring environment which is welcoming and friendly, based upon sound discipline and a structure within which each young person's life can be enjoyable and purposeful.
> Stated simply, our aim here is to enable all concerned to be and to do their best.

Statements such as these reflect what parents want for their children in addition to a well-presented appropriate curriculum. The extract also reflects discussion of the pastoral care system which has been taking place within schools and by observers of school life over the past 20 years. For example, Clemett and Pearce (1986) suggest that pastoral care contains three main elements. These are:

> Helping young people towards achieving the skills and personal qualities which they will need for informed decision making and the acquisition of personal autonomy.
>
> Acknowledging and suitably equipping pupils with the skills required for adulthood.
>
> Providing help, guidance and support in order that children can function effectively in school.

These elements, like those from the school handbook, indicate a concern on the part of the school for pupils' self concept, for their capacity to make and maintain social relationships and for the development of a sense of citizenship. How can the school facilitate the growth of these qualities?

On the one hand, it can be argued, a concern for the development of personal and social attributes should permeate the whole of the school curriculum. Indeed, many schools actively promote the view that all adults and pupils in the school should work together to create a climate where there is a concern for others, awareness of social responsibilities and a willingness to be involved in the community both within and outside the school.

At the same time, all schools set aside time which is specifically devoted to social and personal issues. This may be done in assembly, in form periods, through topic work or, specifically in the secondary school, in Personal and Social Education (P.S.E.) lessons. At its most basic level, this kind of lesson promotes the flow of communication among participants by encouraging group members to share ideas and experiences with one another in an atmosphere which is warm, friendly and accepting, so creating a context where it is possible for pupils to address interpersonal problems, promote cooperative values and develop a sense of social responsibility. Where children are experiencing specific interpersonal difficulties, this kind of classroom work offers a setting in which conflicts can be worked through in a safe environment with the support of peers and a facilitative adult.

From this perspective, the very process of being in a supportive class group can enhance the social and emotional development of the child.

Silveira and Trafford (1988) suggest that, in the case of the child who finds it exceptionally difficult to be accepted in groups (whether in the family, at school or in the peer group) it is usually possible to trace this back to some traumatic event which coincided with a crucial stage in the development of social skills. In their view:

> life events, such as moving home, changing schools, physical illness, separation or loss in the family, etc., etc., occurring at times when the child is just about to negotiate the next rung on the ladder of the group hierarchy, can hinder the child's progress or cause him to regress to earlier and, therefore, inappropriate age behaviours. (p. 1)

These situations are likely to be public knowledge. Children can also, as we know, become distressed through more private interpretations of situations and events. Teachers who take care to create a co-operative climate in their classes can do much to help such children regain a pattern of healthy development.

Personal and Social Education

Teachers of P.S.E., using strategies which have evolved from the person-centred approach advocated by counsellors and psychotherapists, are likely to be concerned with giving their students opportunities to develop confidence, to become trusting of one another, to share personal experiences with other members of the group, and to become more self-aware. The philosophy which underpins this approach is that each person is unique and sees the world in a distinctive way; each person has the capacity to find out what is right for him or her. Many of the techniques which are used are derived from the practice of counselling.

This approach stresses that teachers need to promote, both in themselves and among their students, qualities of empathic understanding, acceptance and genuineness in order to create a learning climate which facilitates personal growth. There are many well established experiential activities which facilitate this. For example, a group of pupils might be encouraged to share feelings in a circle where the teacher would enable the group to feel free to voice feelings without the risk of being ridiculed. In a round, each person might be invited to complete sentences like 'I noticed . . .', 'I wish . . .', 'My greatest fear is that . . .', 'I resent it when . . .' or 'I appreciate it that . . .'

The emphasis is on eye contact, sharing and on the involvement of each person. There are often 'ground rules' where everyone agrees to listen to the speaker without comment. Participants also might agree to respect each person's right to say 'Pass' if they do not feel ready to share thoughts and feelings at a particular moment. This approach can be used for many purposes – for discussing responses to a film or for exploring feelings within the group.

Circle-time is now an established method for promoting self-esteem and positive behaviour in the primary school (Mosley, 1993a; 1993b). Circle-time is best done as a regular part of the school timetable. Teacher and children sit in a circle where all share in the aim of promoting positive behaviour. Activities take the form of co-operative games, role-play, talking and listening exercises, and puppet play. There are ground rules: everyone has a turn; everyone has a right to be heard; there are no 'put-downs'. Circle-time is effective in generating a positive climate in the class. This in turn promotes peer-group pressure for mutually acceptable behaviour.

It is important in all these activities that the teacher does not dominate but models qualities of empathy and of listening supportively. This way of working is now so commonplace in British schools that it is easy to forget that twenty years ago it was virtually unknown, except perhaps in drama lessons and some innovative English lessons. These kinds of behaviour were typically stifled in schools and most pupils learned that it was not appropriate to express feelings in the classroom. In fact, non-expressive, controlling teachers, like other authority figures, were viewed with respect or with fear; if they were emotional and sensitive, they might, it was feared, be viewed with contempt. Rarely would pupils feel able to form a warm, personal relationship with a teacher. It should not be concluded that in British culture young people were not encouraged to express their feelings. Rather that this did not occur in school. Personal feelings and social relationships were 'taken care of' in the family or within the peer group. School was a place where you learned to work.

Philosophies in education change to take account of social and political pressures and directions. It is interesting to speculate on the possible guiding ethos which will pertain in schools in another 20 years time. Will the emphasis on pastoral issues be more prominent even than it is today with schools taking on more and more of the role of equipping young people for citizenship? Will schools be largely pupil governed, following on from our current thinking about children's rights, or will schools have reverted to a solely academic function?

The history of pastoral care

The emphasis on personal growth and on social skills training became prominent in British schools from the late 1970s through the extensive work of the Counselling and Career Development Unit (C.C.D.U.) based at the University of Leeds. This group produced books, curriculum materials and training courses for teachers in the broad area of personal and social education. The process of developing courses which promoted personal skills development among students inevitably challenged traditional, teacher-centred methods of instruction and had an impact right across the curriculum. Concepts drawn from the literature on counselling predominated. For example, in a widely used publication, Hopson and Scally (1981) suggested that self-empowerment is a central feature of personal and social education. Their detailed package of teaching programmes identified key skills for living – 'skills I need to survive and grow', 'skills I need to relate effectively to you', 'skills I need to relate effectively to others' and 'skills I need on specific occasions' (p. 64). At the heart of this programme was a commitment to the view that positive self-esteem is a basis for growth and development and that young people can develop specific social and life skills. The programme required techniques that develop the role of the teacher as a facilitator of others' learning rather than as an expert passing on knowledge of a subject, and it focussed heavily on experiential group work in a whole variety of forms, including discussion, role-play, brainstorming and problem-solving.

This teaching style has been influential in promoting the view that personal and interpersonal experience forms a basis for growth both in the context of personal goals, such as self-confidence and in increasing awareness of how we relate to others in our group. The teacher's role is to facilitate, guide, encourage, and support group members, to enable pupils to explore self in relation to others, and to make ideas and experiences personally meaningful. Pupils are encouraged to be open about expressing their feelings, both positive and negative. There is an emphasis on change, for example when a child who was previously shy and unforthcoming develops social skills in the safety of the group and is empowered to make a short presentation to the class; or when the victim of bullying in the playground is enabled, through the medium of role-play, to share her distress in the group and experience the support of peers. Essentially there is a concern to increase the effectiveness of the person both as an individual and in the context of the group. Values such as autonomy, choice and self-fulfilment are promoted; individuals are given the opportunity to explore new ways of relating to other people; to explore what change means to the person; to change unproductive patterns of behaviour; and to celebrate positive aspects of the self.

However, it would be misleading to suggest that all this innovation has occurred without conflict. Many teachers are still divided in their feelings about the emphasis on personal and social education. Cowie and Rudduck (1988) found that, while most teachers stated that it is important to develop personal qualities in their pupils, at the same time, they expressed strong reservations about the effectiveness of a person-centred approach (p. 59). What they seemed to be expressing was a fear of a breakdown of discipline and a reluctance to let go of the teacher's traditional power and control in the classroom.

The ambiguity and unpredictability which is characteristic of group work of this kind seems to be threatening to many teachers. In addition, there are deeply-embedded traditions in the British educational scene which act against innovations of this kind. On the positive side, it is now the case that all secondary schools have timetabled lessons solely concerned with social and personal education. The quality of interpersonal relationships are now seen as very much the concern of the school.

Care and control

We have been talking about the caring parts of the school community which are usually contained within the academic curriculum. However, since discipline is an issue which is often raised by parents when deciding which school to choose for their child, systems for care and control are also considered separately. The Elton Report (DES, 1989) on discipline in schools highlighted the importance of process skills in the classroom and argued the case for the creation of a school context where quality of relationships and a sense of school community were held to be of value. This is paralleled by the continuing concern by educators, policy-makers, parents and school governors to reduce the incidence of bullying in schools. This is emphasised in recent H.M.I. guidelines for the inspection of schools. For example, schools may now be asked specifically about what action they take to prevent bullying. The Department for Education funded a research project designed to investigate the problem of bullying in school and develop new guidelines for schools on this issue (Sharp and Smith (eds.) 1994; Smith and Sharp, 1994). Interventions include peer-counselling, quality circles where pupils themselves adopt a problem-solving approach to bullying in their own school setting, assertiveness training for victims, the method of shared concern (a therapeutic way of working directly with bullies and their victims), drama and role-play, improved playground environment and supervision – all devised within the framework of a whole-school policy on bullying which has been formulated and negotiated in a co-operative, consultative way with all members of the school community (Sharp and Smith (eds.), 1994; Smith and Sharp, 1994).

Whilst bullying and discipline are whole-school concerns, there are, within each school, identified members of staff who deal with such issues and policies. Discipline is part of the caring function of a school – making it run smoothly; ensuring that all children's rights are met; protecting members of the school community, and expressing care and concern through the establishment of boundaries.

> The pastoral system is concerned with positive forms of discipline which aid the pupil's development of autonomy. (Hamblin, 1978, p. 5)

In fact, the balance between 'care' and 'control' is one of the major factors affecting stress management in teachers (Poppleton et al., 1985), and in pupils.

Best (1989) has constructed a useful model for describing a pastoral curriculum. Here he demonstrates that the pastoral system of a school, exists not only for the pupils, but also for the staff. An effective pastoral system in a school makes life easier for the teachers. The 'pastoral' may be primarily for the pupils, the 'system' primarily for the staff, although both groups have needs in both areas. In Figure 1 Best is talking about curriculum, control, casework and management. Whilst the counselling function seems to fit most readily into the casework category, we suggest that all members of the school community – not only pupils, but also staff or parents, or ancillary staff – could at some point benefit from skilled counselling support.

There is a debate as to whether the pastoral system should be seen as separate from what is often considered to be the normal practice and functioning of the school. Clemett and Pearce (1986) pose the dilemma:

> If it [the pastoral system] is described as separate it appears to be in addition to normal practise but if it is not separately identifiable it is difficult to support and sustain. (p. 14)

Figure 1

Casework Needs of the *child*	**Curriculum** Needs of the *pupil*	**Control** Needs of the *citizen*
– security – warmth – guidance – patience – support – love	Opportunities to – acquire concepts – learn facts – practise skills – develop attitudes	– orderly environment – rules, sanctions – participation – belonging

Educating the *whole person* entails meeting the needs of the individual in all three roles.

FACILITATES

Management
Needs of the *staff*
- Leadership
- Training
- Appraisal
- Appreciation
- Resources
- Inspiration

(Adapted from Best (1989) *The Pastoral Curriculum*)

The identity of the pastoral care system

It is our view that it is in the best interests of the school, the pupils and the staff if pastoral care sustains an identity. But maintaining such an identity need not only be done by teachers with designated posts of pastoral responsibility. In these days of intervention and pressures from central government which have made a particular impact in terms of the National Curriculum, the pastoral side of the teaching role needs to be reviewed.

Kaser (1993) viewed the pastoral system as an 'ecosystem', that is a functioning unit (people) and its environment (the school). This perspective is a useful one as it emphasises the interconnection and interaction of the individual with the environment. Systems theory distinguishes between factors which can and cannot be changed. Within the school situation it is possible, for example, to change the policy on school dress, but not the parents' beliefs on what is an appropriate amount of money to spend on school clothing. Any alteration in the school's policy must therefore take into account external factors. Hobbs (1975), Plas (1986) and others have demonstrated what all teachers know – that a child's behaviour can only be understood adequately if it is viewed as a part of a total network.

This includes good as well as bad behaviour. All too often we evaluate the effectiveness of a school by looking at negative indices such as truancy figures or the incidence of smoking and other aspects of school life which are largely, but not always, under the direct control of the school. A more accurate picture comes from looking at what a school does well not only in terms of academic performance but also in terms of social and emotional performance. For every truant and for every bike-shed smoker, there are dozens who do not abscond or smoke. These factors need to be put into social and statistical perspective. The reality of schools is that they cater to the needs of people who, by and large, conform to acceptable standards in varying degrees. Within these degrees some individuals are more comfortable than others. Those who are less comfortable, or who find conformity unacceptable may require additional help and support. It is within the remit of the teacher to give this.

How do pastoral care issues relate to counselling?

Counselling, as it is discussed in this book, refers largely to a form of relationship between and among individuals. However, a prerequisite for effective counselling is a careful assessment on the part of the teacher of the child's needs and how the school can meet these needs. In addition, an effective pastoral care system will continuously monitor the influence of the school organisation on the social, academic and emotional performance of pupils in addition to encouraging the use of effective techniques for developing personal awareness and skills such as those mentioned earlier.

Teachers are in the best position to undertake systematic monitoring of children's development as, with the exception of the family, children spend more time with their teachers than with any other adults. The influence which schools and teachers have on children should not be underestimated (Blom, Cheny and Snoddy, 1986). The truth of this assertion can be validated if we look back on our own schooling, be it good, bad or indifferent. For most of us, at least one of our teachers has been a significant influence on our development and the way we are today.

Counselling, as we saw in chapter one, is dependent upon the ability and will to listen. To this extent pastoral care issues are directly linked with counselling as both need to take into account what the pupils – both individuals and as a group – say. What do they think they need? What do they think is important? What makes them feel comfortable and respected? Gersch (1992) has written extensively on these concerns. He suggests that systems are likely to be more effective if they encompass pupils' views. Davie (1993) follows on from this argument and says that:

> there is strong and growing evidence in many different spheres as to the efficacy of listening to the voice of the child. (p. 29)

He also points out that the child has the *right* to be listened to.

Young people as active citizens

The Elton Report (DES, 1989) on discipline in schools argued the case for the creation of a school context where quality of relationships and a sense of school community were held to be of value. In order to achieve this aim the Elton Report recommended that head teachers and teachers should recognise the importance of ascertaining pupils' views and should encourage active participation of pupils in shaping and reviewing the school's behaviour policy.

The Government's White Paper *Choice and Diversity: a New Framework for Schools* (DfE, 1992), stated that children should be encouraged to grow up 'as active citizens':

> In a variety of ways and across a range of subject areas, young people should always be taught that, in addition to rights and expectations they also have important duties and responsibilities to their community, they should be encouraged to be involved members of those communities, to grow up as active citizens. They should be taught the importance of developing a strong moral code that includes a concern for others,

> self-respect and self-discipline, as well as basic values such as honesty and truthfulness.

There is no room for complacency, however, argues Newall (1993), chair of the council of the Children's Rights Development Unit. He suggests that while young people's democratic rights may be acknowledged in current legislation, much of educational practice ignores them. Children, in his view, are not given enough scope to make rules and guidelines and to take responsibility for their own school community. Democratic principles, he argues, are the ones most frequently broken in schools. The problem is that many teachers do not trust their pupils to behave responsibly as members of their school community. Yet there is some evidence to suggest that adults frequently underestimate pupils' capacity and willingness to play an active part in promoting positive values amongst their peers.

For example, Salmon and Claire (1984) showed that young people could work collaboratively on issues of common concern in their classrooms provided that there was a willingness to establish common goals and mutual understanding among both teachers and pupils. This process took time and often ran counter to established practice.

Adelman (1989) argued the case for democratic schooling but pointed out the need for teachers to be aware of the difficulties inherent in creating a balance between fostering a pupil's individuality alongside fostering a sense of social responsibility. In his view, there should also be a recognition that the *process* itself is vitally important in giving pupils a meaningful opportunity to reflect on what they do and to consider the impact of their actions on others.

Cowie and Rudduck (1990) showed that, through the process of working collaboratively on a real task such as playing an active part in making choices in P.E., pupils could be given the valuable experience of practical reasoning. In the process of their discussions, the pupils came to understand means in relation to ends, and gained in empathy for the feelings of others as they are affected by the outcomes of a decision-making procedure. They also learned to weigh up alternatives thoughtfully as a way of determining what was right and appropriate. There were useful outcomes from this exercise in practical problem-solving since it enabled pupils to come to a deeper understanding of the principle that responsibility involves not simply getting what is best for oneself but taking into account the perspectives of others. Pupils were thus given the opportunity to develop a sense of concern for others.

In chapter seven we present an account of secondary school pupils working together to set up a peer counselling service to help the victims of bullying. Here we see how pupils themselves were actively involved in the establishment of a pupil-initiated peer counselling service designed to improve relationships at school and specifically to provide a safe place where bullied pupils could talk freely about their experiences and explore possible solutions.

Pastoral care and the teacher

Over the past decade the teaching profession has changed in ethos and career structure. Some would say for the better. If teaching ever was a 'safe' profession with the perks of short hours and long holidays, it certainly is not now. Deciding on a career in teaching is no longer one which can be taken lightly – there are increasing demands and pressures and emphasis on teacher qualifications and post-qualification training. Furthermore, diminished job security, the lessening of personal autonomy in the classroom, diminishing social kudos and contentious pay structures mean that only commitment will suffice. The economic climate of the 1980s and 90s has also meant that teaching is no longer the secure job-for-life which once made it so attractive. Teaching is no longer (if it ever was) a 'soft' option as a career. People enter the profession for many different reasons. For some, their prime commitment is for their subject matter, for others it is a desire to work with children. For all it must be some combination of the two. However, not all teachers are confident in or desirous of working on an intensely pastoral level with their pupils. They may well choose not to engage in individual counselling work with pupils or may feel uncomfortable in this role. The pastoral system needs to acknowledge this and to offer support not only to the pupils, but also to the staff in helping pupils to achieve of their best in the social and personal fields.

The National Curriculum has raised the status of subject specialism within schools. Its emphasis on basic standards means that all pupils can expect to receive a broad and balanced curriculum. This is their right. However, whilst it is now acknowledged that being a good subject specialist is essential, being good with children is also high on teachers' list of priorities. As evidence for this the authors would point to the current increase in teachers opting to train as counsellors or attending counselling courses – often in their own time and with their own money.

Stress in schools

Not all children are happy at school. Some are unhappy because of their personal circumstances; some because of a major or minor event which has befallen them; some because school does not work for them. One of the major factors which influences how comfortable a pupil feels in school is the appropriateness and the delivery of the curriculum – in other words, effective teaching. Another factor concerns clarity of rules and expectations and how consistently these are maintained and administered. One of the major causes of stress is uncertainty.

Another opinion comes from Hamblin (1978) who sees the major stressor in schools as lying in the area of relationships.

> The pastoral team should try to detect, and deal with, problems due to sterile relationships within the school and of inappropriate educational methods. But we must avoid making the pastoral system a mechanism for draining off, in an unthinking way, tensions produced in the school, leaving the real causes untouched. (p. 3)

Lang and Ribbins (1985) found that teachers often underestimated how seriously students perceived problems, and a study by Sharp and Thompson (1992), which looked at teachers' and pupils' perceptions on sources of stress, found a mismatch between what pupils found stressful and what teachers thought they might feel, although there was a divergence of attitudes amongst the different schools in their sample. Aspects of their lives which pupils found stressful were:

- death of a close family member
- illness of a family member
- personal illness or injury
- poor relationship with a teacher
- arguments within the family
- uninteresting lessons
- arguing with friends
- exams
- being told off by the teacher/being in trouble
- difficulty with school work.

As can be seen, more than half of these factors are directly related to school. This study and others like it (for example, Carey, 1993) suggest priorities for the management system of pastoral care.

An earlier study by Lang (1983) found that when asked, pupils said that they thought of the pastoral care system as functioning to resolve problems of control and administration, and few pupils recognised the caring and supportive aspects. However, Clemett and Pearce (1986) found that pupils valued the quality of relationships within a school, particularly those with their peers and 'teachers who display concern, helpfulness, humor and understanding'. The Sharp and Thompson study found that 56 per cent of the children in their sample did in fact value talking to someone about their problems, but this was rarely the teacher. The exception to this was in one of their sample schools where the pastoral system included a good many named pastoral staff including the head teacher. In this school, most of the children who said they would talk to somebody chose a teacher. Other choices of people to talk to were friends and parents. Sharp and Thompson go on to suggest that their results point to the following issues of concern:

- Why do teachers appear to be unaware of many of the stressors experienced by students?
- Is it possible that the students' perceptions of their stressors are in some way biased or incomplete?
- What effects might teacher misperceptions have on teacher judgments and actions?
- What might be the implications of such misperceptions for the management of the pastoral care system?

Which pupils might need help?

Whilst the pastoral system exists for the benefit of everyone, there will be some members of staff and some pupils who need to avail themselves of the facilities of a one-to-one counselling relationship because they are stressed; because they are not functioning or performing adequately; or because they are unhappy in some other way. A proactive system would allow for pupil difficulties to be identified early. Carey (1993) suggests five ways to identify problems which pupils might be having. These are: observation; communication with the pupil; communication with the parents; communication with other sources; and school records.

Observation

This would include observations of behavioural changes, of appearance and of what Carey calls 'covert messages' which are expressed through play, art, drama or creative writing.

Communication with the pupil

Basically, this means talking to the pupil. This type of identification is more likely to occur in an informal setting and need not be with a teacher.

Communication with the parents

The term 'parent' has assumed a wider connotation since the 1989 Children Act, and does not necessarily mean the biological parent. Carey refers to the pupils' 'social parent'. The parent/s may give information directly if they are aware of any problems, or may indicate them indirectly, through discussion of the child's behaviour or attitude or via discussion of their own personal problems. Sometimes the parent is the first to identify a problem, at other times the school invites them to discuss the child.

Communication with other sources

There are ethical issues involved in discussing a child with their friends, relatives, other pupils or staff, but sometimes a teacher makes a judgment that this is in the pupil's best interests.

School records

Records are automatically kept of absences, lateness and illness. Perusal of these records would help to indicate whether the problem is long term or recent.

Many of these points seem obvious, but it is necessary to appreciate that we all express our difficulties in different ways, and just asking someone, or making evaluations as to the reasons behind someone's behaviour can be misleading. Misleading conclusions can be time-wasting and distressing. A strategic and sensitive assessment of the situation will alleviate this. We cannot make assumptions about children's unhappiness from our own personal world-view or perspective. We will discuss this further in chapter five.

Challenges for the pastoral system

Each school is different. The National Curriculum takes little account of these differences in its requirements to deliver academic core subjects. Unlike this academic prescription, each school's pastoral care system will reflect its own unique requirements, community and population. The management of the pastoral system needs, therefore, to be flexible in order to take account of changing social pressures and requirements. This flexibility must include listening to children. Evidence for the efficacy of this is summarised in the Elton Committee's recommendations:

> head teachers and teachers should encourage the active participation of pupils in shaping and reviewing the school's behaviour policy ... to foster a sense of collective commitment to it.

The Elton report was specifically addressing behaviour in schools. We suggest that the above comment is relevant for all aspects of the school's pastoral functioning. Hamblin (1978) says:

> Good pastoral work like good academic work is based upon an open style of thinking which allows one to formulate tentative hypotheses before proceeding to validate them as the evidence emerges. (p. 142)

This flexibility is crucial, because it is not possible to predict the way in which changes in structure or circumstances might affect behaviour and attitudes. For example, a school which decides to move from a linear to a family tutor base may accurately anticipate some of the consequences, both positive and negative. It might also underestimate or overestimate the responses of pupils and staff, and it may completely ignore some aspect of the change which determines the success or failure of the new system. This is because the consequence of changing systems for human relationships is never easy.

> Complex and interconnected processes are influenced by so many variables that their course and final state often cannot be predicted with any certainty. (Dorner, 1989)

Whatever the pastoral system looks like within any school – and all will be different depending on school population, teacher skills, history of the school, make-up of the community etc., – the underlying philosophy will be based on realising the importance of personal development, and preparing pupils for citizenship and life after school.

Conclusions

In this chapter we have argued that the pastoral care system is both a part of, and subsumes, individual counselling within the school setting.

We have used evidence from a good deal of literature and research to illustrate this.

We take the view that effective teacher-pupil relationships and the curriculum can mitigate against many problems which pupils may encounter. Research within schools has identified potential pressure-points within the life of a school and has trialled effective strategies and programmes which teachers can adopt.

We have allowed ourselves a wide definition of counselling to include work done within the classroom with groups of pupils. We think this is valid as, like individual counselling work, these strategies are aimed at promoting the development of self; the development of personal autonomy and responsibility; and dealing with feelings.

Neither pastoral care systems nor counselling relationships can or should ignore the needs and rights of the child.

CHAPTER THREE:

Attachment Theory

Introduction

The counselling approach adopted by teachers with responsibility for counselling in schools is of course influenced by the models which they have experienced during their training. In this chapter, we look at the model of attachment theory which places a strong emphasis on the early years of the person's life and the quality of the relationships which were experienced at that time. From this perspective, the family context into which the child is born has a long-term impact on the development of the child's inner world, sense of self and capacity to form meaningful relationships with others. Attachment theory has grown from the psychodynamic tradition. However, in its most recent formulation, it has also incorporated a cognitive dimension which has important implications for effecting change in the individual's working model of attachment relationships in the present.

Secure attachment

During the past 30 years, researchers and practitioners have documented a significant body of knowledge on the nature and importance of the bond between parents and their children. From this perspective, the concept of attachment integrates social, emotional and cognitive aspects of the child's 'working model' of the relationship between self and others. There are behavioural aspects of attachment designed to maintain and enhance the relationship.

The concept of attachment originated in the work of Bowlby (1958, 1969,1973,1980) to explain the bonding relationship that develops between parents and their infant. (For a useful overview of recent work in attachment theory see Holmes, 1993.) Bowlby viewed attachment as a behavioural system grounded in evolution which had as a set goal the maintenance of proximity to the primary caregiver. In Bowlby's view, separation from the caregiver 'activated' the attachment system in order to restore proximity. During the first year of life, the child's 'proximity-promoting behaviours' such as crying, vocalising, clinging to the caregiver become organised into a goal-oriented system focussed on a specific caregiver, usually, but not necessarily, the mother. When the attachment system has achieved its goal – being in sufficiently close contact with the caregiver – then attachment behaviours subside. The child no longer needs to cry or reach out to the caregiver. In a situation of threat, such as separation from the caregiver or being in an unfamiliar setting or when the child is ill, then attachment behaviours are activated. Then the child will cry, cling, call out and behave in ways which are likely to result in closer proximity to the caregiver.

Here is what a teacher, on a routine visit to a family, might observe as she saw a mother interacting with her one-year-old child.

> Terry, the child, plays as the parent and teacher talk. Every so often he stops in his play and calls out to his mother or points out an object to her. He turns round regularly to look at her; from time to time he runs over to her and stays close before going back to his toys. He does not leave the room where she is sitting. When she goes into the kitchen to fetch some biscuits, the teacher invites him to play with her in a friendly way but Terry looks doubtful and turns away. He then toddles after his mother and holds on to her skirt. When they return to the living room, Terry resumes his play but stays near to his mother.

What is happening here? Terry is using his mother as a secure base from which to explore his world; he reassures himself regularly that she is still there for him. He smiles at his mother and shows some wariness of the stranger. Both adults accept and enjoy the interaction and are able to get on with their business. This is an example of a secure 'attachment relationship'. Scenes like these will be re-enacted many times in the course of Terry's day. 'Attachment behaviour' is characterised by smiling and vocalising preferentially to the caregiver; crying and attempting to follow when this person leaves; greeting, hugging and being comforted when the caregiver returns. In other words, the caregiver is perceived as a secure base from which to explore the environment, and as a place of refuge to return to for comfort when threatened. The relationship is two-way and is mutually satisfying to both parties. The child plays an active part in this process and both adult and child become reciprocally attached. Most of us in our culture will have observed this kind of parenting and enjoyed it, as all three participants in this interaction did.

Bowlby also argued that infants have a predisposition to explore the outside world. The need to explore and play takes the child away from the parents and counteracts the need to be near them. A balance is kept between these two tendencies in which both parent and infant play an active part. The balance shifts when the child is distressed by some event or experience, such as illness or sudden separation from a familiar caregiver. At these times of threat, the infant will cry or cling or show other behaviours which are likely to elicit closer proximity to the caregiver. All parents of toddlers will be familiar with times, for example at the end of the first morning at playgroup, when their children displayed seemingly babyish needs for comfort by clinging or crying or asking to be cuddled. A few weeks later the same child would greet the parent calmly and ask to go to play with a new-found friend.

Bowlby went on to argue that significant separations between the child and his or her primary caregiver (usually the mother) in the first five years of life would have a serious effect on the emotional and social development of the child. But a great deal of research has been carried out since then and most attachment theorists are now convinced that the young child can cope with, and greatly benefit from, a range of close relationships with significant adults. Furthermore, it now seems certain that it is the quality of the relationship with significant caregivers which is the important factor rather than simply the quantity of time spent with them.

Patterns of attachment

Since Bowlby, attachment theory has generated a great deal of empirical research. Ainsworth and her colleagues (1978) developed a method – the 'Strange Situation' – of assessing the attachment between infants and their mothers by observing, in a standardised way, how well the infant uses the caregiver as a secure base for exploration and how well the infant is comforted by the caregiver after a mildly stressful separation. Children who cried during separation from their mothers but who were easily soothed upon reunion were referred to as having a *secure* attachment style. These children were characterised by actively seeking and maintaining proximity, contact or interaction with their mothers, especially in the reunion episode. Any distress expressed by the children during the separation period was clearly related to the mother's absence. By contrast, children who were *insecurely* attached to their mothers responded differently on reunion (see figure 2). Ainsworth's pioneering work identified three distinct patterns of attachment, based on observations of brief separation and reunion episodes involving mothers and their one-year-old infants. In Ainsworth's original study, 65 per cent of the babies showed a secure pattern of attachment (Type B), 21 per cent an anxious/avoidant pattern (Type A) and 14 per cent an anxious/ambivalent pattern (Type C). Main and her colleagues identified a further pattern of insecure attachment which they called disorganised (Type D).

Observational studies of mothers interacting with their babies confirm the experimental evidence. Mothers of securely attached babies are more responsive to cries of distress, smile at their babies more and are more likely to show spontaneous expressions of joy and pleasure in the interactions. Mothers of anxious/avoidant babies are unresponsive to signals of distress, interact less often and show less pleasure in routine care-giving activities. Mothers of anxious/ambivalent babies are unpredictable and inconsistent in their responsiveness to signals of distress and typically wait until the cries have become extremely demanding before they give attention and care. It would appear that mothers of insecurely attached babies show a mismatch in their 'attunement' and sensitivity to the child's needs (Stern, 1985). This in turn has a negative effect on the development of a sense of integrated self in the child.

A meta-analysis of 2000 infants from eight different countries shows a very similar pattern of distribution but there are also cultural differences. Type A children are more common in European countries and in the USA; Type C children are more common in Israel and Japan (Van Ijzendoorn and Kroonenberg, 1988). There are also variations within cultures, for example between families from different socio-economic backgrounds.

The internal working model of relationships

Bowlby suggested that individuals whose caregivers have consistently responded positively to their distress calls develop an 'internal working model' of themselves as worthy of love and see their caregivers as people who are likely to respond to their needs. By contrast, individuals whose caregivers have tended not to respond to them warmly and positively develop models of themselves as unworthy of love and

Figure 2: PATTERNS OF ATTACHMENT
Behaviour of securely and insecurely attached infants during the Strange Situation.

Type A – Insecure attachment: anxious/avoidant attachment style.
Infants who shunned contact with their mothers upon reunion were said to have an *avoidant* attachment style. These infants showed conspicuous avoidance of proximity or interaction with the mother in the reunion episodes. Either the infants ignored the mother on her return or mingled welcome with avoidance responses such as turning away, moving past the mother or averting a gaze. The stranger and the mother were treated in very similar ways throughout the experimental situation.

Type B – secure attachment style.
Children who cried during separation from their mothers but who were easily soothed upon reunion were referred to as having a secure attachment style. These children were characterised by actively seeking and maintaining proximity, contact or interaction with their mothers, especially during the reunion episode. Any distress expressed by the children during the separation period was clearly related to the mother's absence. The child clearly preferred the mother to the stranger.

Type C – insecure attachment: anxious/ambivalent attachment style.
These infants were very upset when the mother left the room but were not easily comforted on her return. They resisted contact but combined this behaviour with some seeking of proximity. Some of these children showed anger at the mother at reunion and gave the impression of being ambivalent about reunions after separations. They also resisted comfort from the stranger.

Type D – insecure attachment: disorganised attachment style.
Main and her colleagues identified a fourth pattern of attachment which they called *disorganised*. The disorganised child appears dazed, confused or apprehensive, and shows no coherent system for dealing with separation and reunion. The disorganised child behaves in seemingly inexplicable ways which suggest fear or confusion about the relationship, for example by 'freezing' on reunion with parent or displaying stereotypical movements.

view their caregivers as unreliable. As the child develops, the goals of the attachment system are modified to allow for greater separation from the caregivers. The child is beginning to develop an internal working model which reflects his or her experiences in relationships. The quality of early relationships influences the child's concept of self as well as attitudes towards others and exisiting expectations of relationships. Thus children who have had a warm, satisfying experience early on in life are likely to see themselves as lovable, appreciate that they are likeable and place a value on close, intimate relationships with others. Those who have had a harsh experience of relationships, who have been rejected, who have not been comforted when in distress are likely to see themselves as unlovable, have low expectations of relationships and act in ways which are likely to elicit rejection.

The pattern seems to endure. Secure pre-schoolers and five- to seven-year-olds respond positively to a parent on reunion and seem to be able to combine attention to the parent with the capacity to explore the environment and relate to other adults and children. Separation is less stressful to these children than it was when they were younger since they seem to have developed an internal working model which assumes that the parent will be there when needed but which allows for reasonable separation, for example when attending nursery or first school, or playing at a friend's house. Reunions are happy and conversation is natural and free-flowing. There is relaxed eye contact and the child may initiate physical contact or nearness. Terry, for example, in later life is likely to maintain the pattern of secure attachment because he feels secure with his primary caregivers. He can separate from them and develop his own style of living. Even the turbulence of adolescence can be understood within the attachment theory framework if we consider the difficulty of the task of separation from parents which the young person must accomplish. As the adolescent tries to disengage from parents, there is also the experience of grieving for the loss of childhood. The transitional period of forming close, intimate relationships within the peer group is not easy, but this task is a normal part of growing up. Likewise, secure adults value relationships and can talk easily about them. If their childhood was secure, they can acknowledge the failings of their parents in an accepting way. If their childhood was difficult, they have worked through their unhappiness and come to an understanding of how it came to happen; they have been able to form new relationships of significance.

The experience of loss

As we have seen, all children have to go through the experience of separation from their caregivers and others to whom they are attached as a normal stage in their development. The need to stay close to familiar, loved ones is counterbalanced by the need to explore new relationships and experiences. It is the way in which the feelings are handled which seems to be the key factor. This is what Ainsworth meant when she described sensitive parenting. Fortunately, most children are supported through their experiences of separation and loss.

Studies by Robertson and Robertson (1971) documented the responses of young children to brief separation from their parents through hospitalisation. These children showed a characteristic sequence of response beginning with protest and prolonged crying, changing to a state of apathetic despair from which they could not be roused, and moving eventually to detachment, an apparent return to normality which masked their deeper feelings. When the parents returned, there would typically be a period of time during which the child rejected them or avoided them before finally accepting that they really had returned. For these children, it seemed, the separation from parents was experienced as abandonment.

If the reunion cannot take place (for example, when parents die) or if the child's feelings are not dealt with, the sense of loss can persist into later life and an insecure pattern for forming relationships with others may be established. This is what seems to have happened to Lesley Brown, a 14-year-old, who was causing her teacher concern:

> Lesley had great difficulty in forming relationships with peers at school and was usually uncooperative and surly. She was often sick. She missed many lessons by spending time in the medical room although there was nothing apparently wrong with her. When Mrs Buck, her teacher, met the parents at a school fair she took the opportunity to talk to them. They had not turned up for their appointment at the parents' evening on the previous week. She told them that Lesley was often alone at school and that she spent time with the school nurse or any other adult who was available.
>
> Mr and Mrs Brown seemed ill at ease with each other. Lesley, too, avoided eye contact with her parents. Mrs Buck noticed that this pattern repeated itself at school. Lesley shied away from contact with her peers; friendships did not last long and seemed to be based on convenience rather than on mutual liking. When Mrs Buck had gently voiced this concern to Lesley, she replied, 'I'm not bothered.'
>
> Mr and Mrs Brown expressed their worries about Lesley but said that they were at a loss over how to help her. Mr Brown reported a similar lack of feeling on Lesley's part, 'We bought her a budgie and she was in charge of it. The other day we found it dead and there was no food or water in the cage. She didn't seem at all upset. All she said was, "Can I have a dog?"'
>
> It emerged that Lesley had been 'difficult' as a baby. In Mrs Brown's words: 'I was ill when Lesley was a baby and I was in hospital for a long time.'
>
> From Mr Brown's perspective:
>
> 'She wasn't easy to cuddle. She wasn't lovable like Marie, our

> other daughter. We do love her but we're not a family to show our feelings.'

One possible explanation for Lesley's current behaviour and attitude could be that she developed an internal working model of relationships based on perceived early rejection by the mother; in time, she became an insecurely attached child who avoided closeness, appeared untouched by rejection and showed dislike at discussing childhood experiences. In chapter six we see how counselling enabled Lesley to change her internal working model of relationships and to change in her feelings about herself.

Dealing with anger

Parents who, however unwittingly, project their own problems on their child are often unpopular with the teacher-counsellor who can see the situation from the outside, but has to be careful not to be judgemental. These parents suffer, but the child who has not worked through feelings of loss from the past is also likely to be angry, and often inappropriately angry in situations which reactivate intense and unresolved emotions from the past. An important part of counselling will be the extent to which this anger can be explored, understood and worked through. Once this has happened, the child is much more able to relate in a realistic way to other people in the present. This does not mean that the child will never be angry again but that the child will be more capable of handling this kind of normal emotional reaction in other situations.

Take the case of Billy whom we will describe next. His attachment to his parents was of the anxious/ambivalent type. Children like Billy remain preoccupied by the relationship with their parents. They will typically engage in long, drawn-out arguments with the parents, are often whiny and clingy. Even by school age, these children are still upset at the prospect of separation from their parents, yet show ambivalence in their presence.

Mr Hall, Billy Hallam's teacher, called on Mr and Mrs Hallam because of his concern. Despite his ability, Billy, aged 9, was making no progress with his reading and his handwriting had deteriorated since first school. He was always quarrelling with his peers and seemed to bear grudges. At break no one would play with him. He was often tearful and unhappy. Mrs Hallam confirmed that 'he is always in trouble on our street':

> 'Billy usually comes in crying and the other day a neighbour complained that Billy had hit her little girl. Billy said that she deserved it because she called him nasty names.'
>
> Mrs Hallam warmed to the subject:
>
> 'There's no peace in our house. Billy picks fights with his brother and sister. He's never happy. All he wants to do is to hang about with me and his dad but he is not pleasant to have around. He complains and whines about everything. We can't even go out for the evening and leave him with a babysitter.'
>
> Mr Hallam went on:
>
> 'He's making our lives a misery, especially his mum. His mum got so desperate she phoned Social Services to have him taken away after he ran away. We were just going down to the pub for a pint. Next thing we knew he'd gone! The police brought him back hours later and said, "You've got a right one here." We are at our wits end. We can't do anything with him and we can't do anything without him.'

The parents went on to describe that Billy, as an infant, was not easily soothed: he had resisted contact with them but was distressed when they put him down. When he got older, he would often challenge his parents and carry on minor disputes with his peers long after the other people had forgotten or forgiven. He had tantrums when he went to first school but seemed all right in the classroom. When he got home, there were more tantrums. A pattern was emerging. He seemed more preoccupied with his relationship with his parents than with other activities. Parent and child engaged in many drawn-out arguments but, at the same time, Billy remained whiny and clingy. Even by junior school age he continued to be upset by separations from his parents.

Counselling work by the educational psychologist with the parents and with Billy – at first separately and then together – helped the family to locate and express the deeply ambivalent feelings they all had towards one another. Billy was able to act out the deep-seated rage he felt towards his parents – but this time within the safety and support of the counselling relationship. Gradually he became more able to relate positively to his peers; parallel to this came a marked improvement in his school work.

How practitioners approach problems

Attachment theory hypothesises that there are continuities between early experience and later relationships. Here the concept of the internal working model offers a helpful strategy for therapeutic intervention. In Bowlby's original formulation, the internal working model was based on the quality of the early relationship between parent and child. It continues to be the view of attachment theorists that through the experiences of relationships with important caregivers the child builds up an expectation of the quality of his or her relationships with other people, including the self. This concept has been widely adopted by counsellors working in the attachment theory tradition. Their emphasis is on unravelling the impact which stressful childhood experiences and unresolved conflicts can have on relationships. In particular, from this perspective, it is held that the repressed conflicts from childhood are likely to be repeated in the next generation unless the individual is helped to work through them. For teachers and other professionals in school settings, the concept of the internal working model offers the prospect of enabling the child to change insecure patterns of relating to others, through the child's experiences of the wider social world, through relationships with adults other than the parents and with peers, or, when appropriate, through counselling.

Counsellors working within an attachment theory framework will create opportunities for the client to explore the inner world of feelings and memories. Clients will be encouraged to look at the loss they have experienced, what this meant and how they responded to it.

The sensitive counsellor uses techniques as appropriate – but the aim is to enable the client to come to understand present-day behaviour in the light of past events. Through the experience of the counselling relationship, the client becomes enabled to deal with highly charged emotional situations in new ways.

How can the counsellor tap into the child's experience of attachment? Talking directly may not always be possible since one of the difficulties may be that the child is reluctant to talk about feelings, in part through embarrassment, in part through a denial and avoidance of painful emotions. Effective techniques include telling stories, using imaginative play, drawing, engaging in talk through doll or puppet play; with older children and adolescents these techniques continue to be helpful in the context of talking through the issues of concern. Such projective techniques enable the child to explore painful memories and experiences in a safe context.

Silveira and Trafford (1988), working with small groups of primary school children who had recently suffered loss through family breakdown, describe how they used the 'Family Sculpt' technique to help children to acknowledge their feelings about parental separation. Children sit in a circle and are invited to 'sculpt' their family with chairs. As many chairs are placed in the circle as there are members of the child's family. The child arranges them in relation to the closeness of family members to one another; alternatively, if the chairs are coloured, they can represent different moods. Each child in the group is given fifteen minutes to arrange the chairs. The teacher stands near the child to give non-verbal support and to clarify any feelings which may emerge. Once the child has completed the sculpt, he or she is asked to talk about it with the group. Members of the group can ask questions about the sculpted family.

This method is useful because, in the process of making the 'Family Sculpt', the child can clarify feelings about the separation. The group leader can use the activity to facilitate discussion in a supportive, trusting group context. The activity encourages communication and allows children to understand that others have very similar feelings of anger, sadness and hurt.

CHAPTER FOUR:

Rational Emotive Therapy

Introduction

In the previous chapter we were introduced to two children who were having difficulties, Lesley and Billy. A probable explanation for their current unhappiness was given in terms of attachment theory. We will now ask some different questions to try to understand these two pupils in order to move towards an alternative form of explanation – Rational Emotive Therapy (R.E.T.).

In the case of Lesley the first question must be to ask who owns the problem? Is it Lesley, or does ownership more appropriately lie with those who are close to and care about her, such as her parents or her teachers. Maybe Lesley really 'isn't bothered', as she says herself. However, let us assume that Lesley is not a contented young person. She certainly appears ill at ease with others and her behaviour suggests someone who is confused about her feelings. It is not hard to accept the attachment theory interpretation of Lesley's early childhood experiences – particularly her early separation from her mother – as having a direct bearing on her current emotional state and behaviours. However, we then need to go on to ask what is going on in Lesley's mind to maintain her unhappiness. What is it about Lesley – about the way she thinks, feels and behaves which makes it difficult for her to have friends or to get close to people?

In the case of Billy, again, there are some practical considerations to take into account. The first question must be about the appropriateness of the curriculum which he is experiencing. Is school such a miserable place for him that he takes out his frustrations at home? We have enough evidence to suggest that Billy's difficulties are multi-faceted and deep-seated. He cries and has no friends. Also, he seems to be preoccupied with his parents in an unhappy, confrontational way. This is not a happy or a useful state for a 9-year-old child – or, for that matter, for a child or adult of any age. Once we have ruled out environmental factors, this remains the most feasible issue to address: what is happening in Billy's head for him to be so unhappy?

In this chapter we will look at an explanation of human unhappiness from a cognitive stance, more specifically from a Rational Emotive Therapy perspective.

Rational Emotive Theory (R.E.T.) has as its basic philosophy the quotation from Hamlet: 'There is nothing either good or bad but thinking makes it so', or, to explore the historical note further, from the Greek philosopher Epictitus who says: 'Man is not disturbed by events, but by the view he takes of them'. In other words, we feel what we think.

This basic premise was adopted by Albert Ellis in the 1950s when he explored the potential of human thought as a major counselling tool. He began his career as a counsellor, working as a clinical psychologist in America. He followed the psychoanalytic school of training but became dissatisfied with both the process of psychoanalysis and its results. He became convinced that it is our thoughts which form the root of human distress and unhappiness.

Rational Emotive philosophy and practice grew from a combination of learning theory and behaviourist approaches, as Blackburn (1986) suggests, 'more an evolution than a revolution'. Proponents of R.E.T. believe that it stands on its own as a philosophy, as a theory and as a basis for counselling.

Rational Emotive Therapy in its purest form gives no credence to theories which emphasise the overriding significance of early developmental experiences and relationships. It suggests that whilst our upbringing and our early childhood feelings do, undoubtedly, play a large part in determining the personalities which we adopt as adults, these ways of thinking, feeling and behaving need not stay with us. We are all, as unique individuals, powerful in terms of being able to shape our behavioural and emotional reactions.

Unlike attachment theory, Rational Emotive Theory does not place great emphasis on the causal factors behind our distress. However, it does acknowledge the importance of environmental and historical factors in terms of our personal histories, but does not use them as the starting point for counselling or therapy. This is because of the belief that by concentrating on bad experiences of the past we are encouraging ourselves to think irrationally, that is, engage in a form of emotional self-indulgence – and this in itself can lead to continuing self-fulfilling misery. Instead, the counselling would help clients to look at their own rules for living. Many of these rules will illustrate the irrational and self-fulfilling nature of the way we treat ourselves.

Basically, R.E.T. moves away from the idea that we are controlled by our feelings – that our feelings are like monsters which come from nowhere and devour us. Sometimes, of course, when dreadful or distressing things happen to us, such as a bereavement or other loss, our emotions rise, quickly and unbidden, to the surface, and dominate our thinking and our lives. This extreme sadness or anger is appropriate. However, it is only appropriate for a period of time. The consequences of being stuck with strong emotions over a long period of time is debilitating, and affects both our thoughts and our behaviours. Such extreme outcomes of upsetting experiences are not, says R.E.T., inevitable or necessary. A rational emotive outlook puts the thinking human being in the driver's seat. It is an empowering philosophy and an effective therapy.

Philosophical underpinnings and interpretations

We are all philosophers in that we all think about our thinking, even though for most of the time most of us do not know we are doing it. This idea gained acceptance following the writings of George Kelly (1955) who believed that we are all scientists in that we make and test out hypotheses in order to reach satisfactory explanations and conclusions about the way we behave in the world. Rational Emotive Therapy uses this basic belief in its explanations of why we are often unhappy and feel that we need help. However, even the best philosophers do not always think rationally: R.E.T. states that we arrive at our irrational beliefs by various routes, none of which have scientific validity as they cannot be proven. That is, we are not given our beliefs in the way we are given hair colour or size; rather, we inculcate them into our world-view for various reasons – usually reasons of habit, or because the pay-off for being unhappy and miserable is seen as, in some way, being rewarding. Some irrational beliefs are maintained because they were at one time true, for example 'my mother rejected me'. This is commonly transferred into an enduring belief that everyone will reject me, even though there is no proof that this is the case.

We hang on to our irrational beliefs even when they are no longer appropriate. This prevents us from developing as autonomous self-directed human beings and causes us unhappiness.

Rational Emotive Therapy postulates that the ability to be irrational is a natural human characteristic in that it is something which we all, at some time, engage in. As Ellis (1984) says:

> 'Even if everybody had had the most rational upbringing, virtually all humans would often irrationally escalate their individual and social preferences into absolutistic demands on (a) themselves, (b) other people and (c) the universe around them'. (p. 20)

The word 'rational' in R.E.T. terms has a slightly different meaning from that which we usually expect: it refers to those mental processes which help people to achieve what they want – their goals – and 'irrational' means that which *prevents* them from achieving these goals. The word 'rational' has further difficulties in that it is often associated with 'unemotional'. Within the R.E.T. framework this is certainly not the case. R.E.T. does not suggest that all emotions are unhelpful, but rather that the frequency, intensity and duration of extreme emotions which do not lead to personal fulfilment or help us to move forward and develop our full human potential are often damaging and inhibiting, and are caused not by the event itself, but by the way we are thinking.

Goals of Rational Emotive Therapy

The goals of a rational approach are summarised by Walen, DiGuiseppe and Wessler (1980) as follows:

- survival
- achieving satisfaction with living
- affiliating with others in a positive way
- achieving intimate involvement with a few others
- developing or maintaining a vital absorption in some personally fulfilling endeavour.

We look now at some of the basic cornerstones of Rational Emotive Therapy.

1. Response options

There are only four possible ways of responding both psychologically and practically to a problem. These are: (a) change; (b) avoid; (c) do nothing; (d) accept.

To take the example of a pupil, let's say Terry, a happy, well-adjusted child – now 14 years old – who has just taken a science exam and received a lower mark than expected in this area. What could he do and what is he likely to be thinking?

(a) He could attempt to *change* the situation by direct methods such as persuasion or argument. In the case of the low mark in the test he could confront the science teacher who marked the exam, or approach the head of department or write to the DfE complaining about the rigours of the National Curriculum.

(b) He could *avoid* facing the situation. In this case, the situation (the low mark) has already happened, but he can avoid the consequences by distracting or diversionary strategies such as overeating; drinking; throwing himself into an alternative activity; or pretending that the low mark didn't really happen.

(c) He may decide to *do nothing* about the situation, put up with it and remain very disappointed.

(d) He could *accept* that for the time being, there is nothing he can do, and instead will look to find effective and constructive ways of reducing his feelings of disappointment. This is the R.E.T. option.

With option (d) Terry would be actively engaged in reducing the emotional, and sometimes behavioural, consequences of his disappointment. He would do this by looking at his *Irrational Beliefs* (I.B.s).

2. *Irrational Beliefs*

A belief is said to be irrational if it is untruthful or unhelpful. These beliefs maintain negative emotions. For example, if Terry is saying to himself: 'this is dreadful' or 'I can't stand being a failure', or 'I ought to have succeeded' then he is likely to be making himself feel not only disappointed – which is appropriate – but guilty, angry and resentful.

Phrases such as those suggested above contain four components. These are:

Demandingness – 'I ought to have succeeded.'
Awfulising – 'This is dreadful.'
Can't stand it – 'I can't bear to be a failure.'
Negative evaluation – 'I'm (or you're) a dreadful person.'

For as long as he thinks like this Terry will not be able to move on to take constructive action or adopt useful thoughts about the event and is likely to feel very miserable and to behave in a way in which miserable people behave.

Dryden (1990) proposes a matrix to describe those components of our thinking about the world which cause us discomfort: The matrix looks like this:

Figure 3: DISCOMFORT MATRIX

	Ego Disturbance	Discomfort Disturbance
I must	A	B
You must	C	D
Life conditions must be	E	F

'Ego Disturbance' means making demands about yourself which result in disappointment. 'Discomfort Disturbance' is similar, but refers to the way the individual feels about that disappointment. In effect, Rational Emotive theory proposes a two-stage model whereby we become disturbed not only by the feelings which our thoughts lead to, but also by the way we think about our feelings.

In the above diagram A, C and E indicate Ego Disturbance. In A, the disturbance comes about through demands towards the self. For example Terry might say 'I must get a good mark or I am no good'. In C, through demands towards others, which would be characterised by 'You should have given me a better mark and the fact that you haven't means that I'm hopeless', and in E through demands about life conditions – 'The exam should have been easier.'

B, D and F on the other hand suggest Discomfort Disturbance towards self, others and life conditions. With B, Terry might be saying 'I must do well at school all the time otherwise my life will be a mess'. With D, 'The teachers should have been more generous with my marking and I can't stand it that they think I didn't do well'. On the other hand, in F he would be saying 'I must not get poor marks because I can't stand it.'

Of the four components mentioned above 'demandingness' and 'extreme negative evaluation' are likely to be the most dominant.

The demand elements will contain such strictures as 'I must succeed'; 'It's got to happen like I want it to', etc. Demand statements contain words such as 'must', 'ought', 'need'.

The 'extreme negative evaluation' component is characterised by phrases such as 'It's dreadful', 'I'm a worthless person', etc. These are worst-thing-in-the-world statements.

Where, asks R.E.T., is the proof behind any of these statements of self-talk? Where is the proof that things must be as we want them, or that you are worthless because you didn't get the mark you wanted, or that this is the worst thing that could happen? The answer is that there is no proof. There is no universal definitive proof that because you failed your exam you are a worthless person. Neither is there proof that things *must* be as you would like them to be. These unfortunate and unpleasant incidents are part of the cause and effect nature of living in the world. Some things go well for you, others less well, others go really badly.

Of course there are implications in helping others to come to terms with the fact that things are not as they would like them to be. As counsellors, we need to guard against the danger of minimising the interpretations which others put on their own experiences. We will deal with this issue further in the chapter on ethics (chapter five).

The negative consequences of a situation or of one of your actions does not make you a negative or a bad person It is just not true and it is not helpful to carry this belief around as an absolute truth. More helpful is the notion of 'responsible hedonism'. This means being happy or contented with the way you are whilst at the same time acknowledging that you are not perfect and neither is the world around you.

'Enlightened self interest' is another R.E.T. concept which advocates feeling comfortable and confident enough in yourself to be able to make choices which please you whilst at the same time considering others. You may choose to put someone else's desires before your own because that is what you really want and you have judged that their needs and desires are of primary importance and that yours are not.

Ellis identified 12 common Irrational Beliefs to which we all succumb at some time or another. These are:

- It is an absolute necessity for me to be loved and approved of.
- I *should* be thoroughly competent and achieve in everything I do.
- Some people are bad and wicked and *should* be punished.

- It is awful if things do not go the way I want them to.
- My unhappiness is caused by things or people and I cannot control them.
- I *must* be terribly concerned about things which may be dangerous or fearsome.
- It is easier to avoid responsibility and difficulties than to face them.
- I need someone or something stronger or greater than me to rely on.
- Things which have affected my life in the past *should* continue to affect me.
- What other people do is of central importance to my existence and I should make great efforts to change them to be more like the people I would like them to be.
- There *must* always be a right answer and it is vital that I find this perfect solution.
- I have no control over my emotions and I cannot help feeling certain things, for example 'You made me love you.'

This, say the proponents of R.E.T. is not an exhaustive list. We could all think of our own favourite Irrational Beliefs which could be added.

All these statements contain either a demand component or an extreme negative evaluation. Some contain both. Ellis suggests that if a person holds vigorously to one or more of these beliefs they will experience not only distress and unhappiness but also a low tolerance for ambiguity; a self-interested frame of mind with little social responsibility; 'awfulise' their experiences and rarely appreciate or accept feedback.

Rational Emotive Therapy engages in the process of changing these Irrational Beliefs (I.B.s) into Rational Beliefs (R.B.s). This is done by a process of *disputing* the I.B.s and thereby achieving a more useful and less distressing emotional life. Following the disputation the process of R.E.T. focusses on recognising the *effects* of this dispute in terms of both feelings and behaviour.

3. The A, B, C, D, E analysis

Thoughts, feelings and actions are, we have seen, closely interlinked within this philosophy. They are all addressed in the A, B, C structure which is a system for analysing a problem.

A is the **Activating** event. In our example 'A' is the low mark.
B is the **Belief** of self-talk.
C is the **Emotion**.

In our example Terry is, as we have already established, feeling defeated, distressed and is experiencing self-doubt and probably anger. R E T stresses the fact that it is not the 'A', which has caused the 'C', i.e. it is not the exam failure which has caused the distress and anger, it is the 'B' – the Belief. If Terry is languishing in 'demandingness' and 'extreme negative evaluation' self-talk then, of course, he will be distressed and angry. This is where the 'D' comes in.

D is the process of **Disputing**.
E is the new **Emotion** or **Effect**.

The 'D' or Disputing would involve questioning along the lies of 'Why is it so awful?' and 'I think I could have been given a higher mark, but these injustices often occur in life.' The Effects, the 'E's of this Disputing are a new Emotion or Effect such as 'It's disappointing and it would have been more pleasant had I got a higher mark, but it's not the end of the world and I may need to take some guidance on my exam technique.'

Changing from Irrational to Rational Beliefs does not entail minimising feelings or consequences, or taking false-comfort from the situation. It means interpreting distressing events in a more positive light which does not bring your whole universe crashing down.

4. The R.E.T. counselling process

A counsellor using an R.E.T. perspective would aim to teach the client that there is no mystery in the process. Together, the client and counsellor would explore the clients Irrational Beliefs and the 'demand' and 'extreme negative evaluation' components and help them to do this for themselves. They would also work together to dispute and substitute the Irrational Beliefs for more rational ones.

The process of disputing Irrational Beliefs can be tuned to fit the linguistic competence, general ability level and age of the client. There are six basic components involved. These are as follows:

1. Recognise what the belief is (for example, 'I'm not a nice person because people keep picking on me') and further recognise that it *can* be changed.

2. Tell yourself to *stop* acting or thinking on the basis of this belief – it is not doing you any good. ('I must have better thoughts about myself because I'm unhappy thinking the way I am.')
3. Substitute a *new*, more rational belief that you can believe in. ('I'm not a horrid person – some people like me and I'm good at maths.')
4. *Act* in the light of the new belief. ('I'm not going to hide myself in the toilets during breaktime – I'm going to find people to talk to.')
5. Continue to *behave* in this new way even though it feels hard. ('I feel awkward and don't know what to say but I'll carry on doing it.')
6. Throughout, believe that things *will* get better. They really do. ('Lesley and Pat asked me about my new bike. I didn't think they were interested. Perhaps they'll come and talk to me tomorrow.').

Richard is a Year 8 pupil. Whilst never particularly keen on school, he was starting to show worrying signs of not wanting to come at all, and was constantly in matron's room complaining of minor ailments. Eventually he confided to his parents that he felt that he had no friends; that his classmates actively excluded him from their activities; and that they laughed at his lack of academic prowess. This was very distressing for all concerned. Not only was Richard's situation distressing, it was also frustrating, as his teachers did not witness the exclusion and ridicule that he described. Richard was only too happy to accept counselling from a member of staff whom he trusted. The first few sessions consisted of Richard giving detailed descriptions of a catalogue of incidents, events, comments and failures which he had experienced. The counsellor ended up feeling jaded, annoyed and powerless. It would have been easy to have spent several sessions discussing Richard's misery – he had the material and the skills to relate it. Instead, the counsellor adopted a Rational Emotive perspective, and by following the six stages, was able to support Richard in being more positive about his situation.

It took two further sessions to get Richard to accept that his Irrational Belief was that everybody should like and approve of him all the time, and if they didn't then life was dreadful and he was hopeless (stage one).

It took a further three sessions to persuade him that it is possible to put different interpretations on other people's behaviour and that other people's behaviour and opinions are not, in any case, so important (stage two).

A further session – and some time which Richard took off school – was needed for him to recognise this and to acknowledge that he was not a failure just because someone laughed when he got an answer wrong (stage three).

With his counsellor, he did some non-threatening role-play of getting an answer wrong (stage four). He was able to laugh at the others (in effect, one person), and also laughed at himself!

He has, since this time, attended school regularly and has said that he does have some friends who play football with him, and they don't like the people in the class who make fun of other people. He is still not enthusiastic about school, and is self-conscious about his difficulties in certain subject areas, but he acknowledges that it is bearable (stage five).

He now tells his counsellor that he hardly recognises his old self (his old feelings), and that whilst he continues to have difficulties, he also continues to play with his friends and is attending school regularly (stage six).

Not only is Richard now more content with his lot, but his counsellor feels that something has been achieved. This is not to say that all is perfect. Perfection is not in the nature of humankind. Richard will still find any excuse not to go to the lesson which he finds the most difficult; his parents still worry about him; and his teachers are vexed by his attention-seeking demands on them. But it is bearable. The old emotion – the extreme unhappiness – is not there any more.

Most children will be able, at their own level, to grasp the logic of this six-stage process. Of course, it may well take time. It will certainly take perseverance and patience. Some children, and quite a lot of adults, think they have a vested interest in maintaining their behaviours and their beliefs even though they make them unhappy. For example, some people behave like victims, and so consequently fall prey to bullying, intimidation and hostility. But being a victim carries a certain status. Such children, and others like them, need to be encouraged to identify and acknowledge the status which they give themselves, and thereby put the opinions of others into perspective (more of this in chapter seven).

How you get the message across is up to you, but one useful technique is to use Rational Emotive Imagery. There are five stages to this:

1. Imagine you are in a situation which you are most worried about (e.g. the playground), and further imagine it in the worst possible way (somebody calls you 'smelly').
2. Focus on how you feel – your emotions (fear, etc.)
3. Re-imagine the same situation, in the same detail – but –
4. Within this situation, with the same thing happening, imagine yourself feeling different (angry with them; furious etc.)
5. Substitute a more rational emotion for the one you first had – this will probably be somewhere in the middle of the current emotion and the feeling you imagined (annoyance; displeasure etc.) Tell yourself that this is a better way to feel.

This is more than a word-game for the emotionally aware. It is a successful and powerful technique which can be learned quickly. Try doing it for yourself, on yourself.

Whilst all counselling is essentially a 'wordy' process, and R.E.T. is sometimes criticised for being more wordy than most, it is still a useful approach for young people and children where techniques and strategies such as imagery and metaphor can be utilised to put across the message of changing your thinking in order to change your emotions and behaviours.

In fact, R.E.T. theory sets out very few specific techniques. It can be practised using a variety of therapeutic styles and approaches, and whilst any form of counselling needs to take into account the developmental level of the client, R.E.T. can, as with any approach, be easily adapted to work with children. All that is required is a grasp of the theory and philosophy and some imagination. The following approaches and techniques are useful in challenging young people's Irrational Beliefs:

1. Help children enjoy their childhood: the fun of games, of taking part in co-operative games. You do not have to win to have fun or to feel valued.
2. Teach young people that most worthwhile goals take time to achieve. Sustained effort is a personal strength.
3. Young people need help to learn that failure to succeed in a goal does not make you bad or worthless. Just because you're not getting what you want, does not mean you're not getting what you need.
4. Help young people to learn that you do not have to be perfect

to be worthwhile. We all have the right to get things wrong. Getting it wrong is part of the learning process.

5. Nobody needs to be liked by everyone to be a worthwhile person. Popularity and 'worthwhileness' are not directly related.
6. Young people need to learn to not take themselves and situations too seriously. We each have the right to be who we are.

As with all psychological theories and practices of counselling, the R.E.T. perspective of viewing and dealing with issues and problems will not suit all clients or all counsellors.

CHAPTER FIVE:

Ethical Issues in Counselling

Introduction

In this book we view counselling as a form of moral dialogue in which both counsellor and client engage, and in which each is potentially active in a process of learning and change. (This does not mean that neither has moral values.) This stance acknowledges that beliefs are shaped by culture, by historical events, by community values, by one's own race and gender, and by one's position in society. Because we live in a society which is culturally diverse, there is not one single moral code by which to live. We argue too that it is impossible not to bring moral considerations into counselling, since many of the issues which are addressed in counselling concern moral decisions: 'I'm pregnant. How can I tell my mum?'; 'Why did my dad leave home?'; 'How could God let my little brother die?'; 'Why do I hate my sister? She can't help being disabled'; 'I think I may be gay. How do I tell my friends?'

The authors found this a difficult chapter to write for many reasons. Firstly, the area of ethics falls within the remit of philosophy and philosophers. We are not philosophers. Like you we are practitioners. Secondly, in their struggle to come to grips with ethics, philosophers have been searching for some universal truths, in other words definitions which hold true over all situations. In reality, people do not work like this. We all follow our noses and our noses are all different. Thirdly, we come up against the complexities of human existence which are particularly evident when we talk about the realms of counselling. Fourthly, because of the complexity of individuals and their relationships, and the way these relationships are positioned within the counselling situation, issues about divided and competing needs are highlighted.

One of the major considerations which we, as adults, need to address in our counselling work with children is the fact that they are often 'sent' for counselling because someone has identified that they have a problem. Whilst this situation sometimes also occurs in work with adults, for example, when they have been referred for 'treatment' by the courts, the prescription of counselling for children and young people, particularly in the school setting, is common. This is a difficult point from which to start.

Counselling is about change – personal change – and as such we cannot, and should not, talk in terms of enforcing counselling on others. It is almost impossible to make people change the more fundamental aspects of themselves *unless they want to*. It is also unethical to try to impose such change on another person. This is allied at worst to brainwashing or intimidation, and at best to social control. Yet counselling, if it is to be effective, is about the process of influencing change. This is a powerful position to be in and it is important that counsellors be aware of the responsibility to facilitate change without imposing their own values on the client. Consider the following situation:

> The realisation that there was a moral dimension to my work as a form teacher came to me forcibly as I struggled to weigh up the needs and rights of the children in my class. Garry was involved in merciless teasing of Alex, a small shy boy in the class. Yet at the same time I knew that Garry was seeing a lot of violent behaviour at home as his parents were frequently engaged in quarrels and recriminations about the past. When Garry's dad walked out after a very bad row, he threatened never to come back. Garry was devastated and his aggressive behaviour increased. I asked Garry's dad to come in to see me. I wanted so much to tell him that it was wrong to desert his family. But he obviously didn't like what he heard. I thought then that the best thing to do was to give Garry time to talk through his problems. I was sure that I was helping him; I also imagined that I was helping Alex indirectly. It was only afterwards that I realised how rejected Alex had felt. To him, my support of Garry was a betrayal, and he became more withdrawn and isolated. (Mrs Jones, a form teacher.)

Mrs Jones in the extract above was describing a very common dilemma faced by counsellors. How do we weigh up the emotional and social needs of children and their families? How do we decide who is responsible for actions which are causing harm or unhappiness to others? How do we judge the outcomes of our interventions on others? What do we do when our own personal belief systems are challenged by those of others? In this chapter, we outline some of the ethical issues which will inevitably confront teachers who engage in counselling as part of their work.

Some counsellors claim to adopt a 'non-judgemental' stance towards their clients' problems. Their view would be that it is inappropriate to apply moral standards to clients' emotional and behavioural difficulties and that their task, as counsellors, is to enable the client to move towards a solution of the problem which is right for him or her. Perls, for example, is famous for his maxim: 'I do my thing and you do yours. I am not in this world to meet your needs, and you are not in this world to meet mine.' (Of course, teachers *do* spend their time meeting the needs of others – teaching is about meeting needs. Perls however is referring not to the academic or social aspects of the human agenda, but to the personal inner world of the individual.)

Such counsellors would deliberately never use the words 'should' or 'ought' in their encounters with clients and would recommend Mrs Jones to make tentative statements like: 'I wonder if you have considered the sadness which you will feel if you continue to do that ...'; or 'It sounds as if you are feeling angry about something ...' Regardless of her own views on how parents ought to act towards their children, she would not pass judgement in any way.

Other counsellors consciously incorporate morality into their helping work with clients. Counselling to them is a form of moral education. Doherty (1993) argues that counsellors must bring ethical considerations into their work and that even those who avoid the words 'ought' and 'should', 'right' or 'wrong' are still taking a moral stance. He writes:

> Our therapy caseloads are like Shakespearean dramas suffused with moral passion and moral dilemmas. But we have been trained to see Romeo and Juliet only as star-struck, tragic lovers, while failing to notice that the moral fabric of parental commitment was torn when their families rejected them because of whom they loved.

He might point out to the family of Garry that their actions were making their child very disturbed and that Garry in particular was becoming more aggressive as a direct result of his father's threat to leave home. He would be likely to suggest to Garry's father that his actions were irresponsible – or even wrong!

Counselling and the law

The law does not ensure that practitioners behave ethically but it does identify areas of concern which are subject to the law and to which legal sanctions can apply. This includes aspects of the client/therapist relationship and the protection of client records (Data Protection Act). So far as work with children in schools is concerned the 1989 Children Act guides and affects our counselling relationships with children so far as disclosure of abuse or likely abuse is concerned. The act requires all local authority agencies to work *together* in the best interests of protecting the child. This means that teachers are legally obliged to share their knowledge of abuse or significant harm with other agencies – usually social services.

The Children Act prescribes the limits to confidentiality. Teachers who are engaged in counselling relationships with children and young people need to be aware of this, and to make the limits of confidentiality clear to the client. Teachers are *not* part of the investigatory process so far as suspected abuse is concerned. They are, however, joint partners in protecting the child.

Most local education authorities specify that a Child Protection Liaison Co-ordinator will be nominated in each school. This is usually one of the senior management team. The function of this role is to advise teacher colleagues as to procedures and to liaise with the other agencies.

Fortunately, teachers are rarely put in the difficult situation of receiving outright disclosures of abuse from children, but teachers are often the first to notice signs of abuse or unhappiness. If abuse or significant harm are suspected, it is mandatory for the teacher to pass on her or his suspicions to the appropriate social services department, who will advise and act appropriately.

The Butler-Sloss report which followed on from the Cleveland enquiry led to the establishment of the Memorandum of Good Practice which sets out the conditions and situations in which children can give evidence in the event of a prosecution against a perpetrator. So far as legal testimony is concerned, there must be no indication that the child has been primed or tutored in their responses. Conversations which a child or young person has had within a counselling situation with a teacher could very well be construed as priming or tutoring. It is therefore neither appropriate nor in the child's best interests for a teacher, on receiving a disclosure, actively to encourage the child to talk further. Any such disclosure interviews must be conducted by the police and social services.

Of course, this is a controversial issue for those of us in the helping professions. Sinanson (1993) argues strongly that, particularly in the case of severely disabled children, allowing them the opportunity to express their distress should be the prime motivating consideration. However, we suggest that one of the skills of counselling is to know when to pull back.

So far as significant harm/abuse is concerned, the law has now taken over, and counselling interventions need to be seen as a part of the process of protecting and supporting the child. The teacher who suspects abuse should set in motion the mechanisms for investigation and should *not* attempt disclosure work within the school setting.

Morality

As adults, and particularly as teachers, we are in a situation which requires us to make decisions for the children in our care. We make these decisions based on our training, our experiences and our inclinations. One of the experiences which we all have in common is the experience of being children. We know what it feels like – at least we know what *we* felt like to be a child. This experience affects our judgement about how the child in front of us may be feeling. These judgements may well be accurate or appropriate. Our training and our experiences have helped us towards this sensitivity. There is, however, inherent in this common experience of childhood, the danger of misinterpreting and minimising the effects of incidents and individual history. For example, you may believe that Terry who is unhappy at not getting a good mark in a test, is overemphasising and over-reacting to what is, in effect, a minor blot on an otherwise good academic record. Or, I may believe that the child who looks hungry and unwashed must be unhappy at home. Yet, we must be mindful that this is *our* belief and not necessarily the belief of the child. The reality is that we cannot judge or quantify the extent of someone's unhappiness or their feelings or interpretations of their own lifestyle. We can make well-defined clinical judgements but we then have to believe the other person's interpretation. This brings into play issues surrounding *truth* and what it means in a counselling situation.

Counsellors need to be aware of the moral conflicts which their clients experience. They must be aware of the values and judgements which they bring to the counselling situation. This does not mean that the counsellor should be morally neutral, even if that were possible. Quite the contrary! The counsellor needs to be attuned to his or her moral values and to understand where their origins are. Counsellors also need to be accepting of the fact that their values may be different from those of their clients. This is especially true when teachers are involved in transcultural counselling and counselling pupils on issues around sexuality and sexual orientation.

Truth and lies

When we describe the way we feel to someone else we usually start by giving information regarding the situation or the setting. In Terry's case the truth is that he did not do very well in an exam. However, this is not, in itself, a truth – it is an interpretation of a fact. The fact is the low mark – the truth is that Terry feels bad about it. You may not feel bad about it, and you may not think that Terry should feel bad either, but the real truth is that he does. This needs to be believed.

Adults involved in counselling relationships with children often become confused or concerned when the young person's description of events does not hold water: the suspicion is that the young person may be lying. Why, the hard-pressed teacher/counsellor may say, would anyone lie in a counselling relationship? Surely such a relationship is based on mutual respect, trust and acceptance. Am I failing in my role if this young person is not telling me the truth about simple facts? Without wishing to give simplistic interpretations, the basic answer to this must be 'no'. We all lie for different reasons. See, for example, the column in a popular newspaper which, each week, asks a celebrity to answer some questions about themselves. One of these questions is 'Under what conditions would you lie?' The answers span the entire spectrum of human analysis and interpretation. With children, reasons for lying are even more complex, as we need to consider the added dimensions of power and subservience in child/adult interactions. If a child or young person lies about a fact or event, there is a reason for it. The lie might be deliberate, it might be to fend off a punishment or reprimand, it may be an artefact of that individual's interpretation, it may be for attention, or for a host of other reasons. Within the acceptance of a counselling situation that lie becomes a reality – it is not a reflection of the counsellor's skills or worth. Challenging perceived untruths is not likely to be helpful in terms of promoting personal growth. It is for the individual concerned to identify their own truths, and a counselling relationship can help to achieve this.

Codes of practice

Many people who are involved in counselling or pastoral care work belong to a professional association, such as the British Association for Counselling, which has a code of ethical conduct (B.A.C., 1984). It is advisable to be familiar with such a code which will offer practitioners some guidance and ensure some protection for clients. However, a word of caution is necessary: *specific* rules of professional conduct are unlikely to be helpful in dealing with complex, real-life situations in which people have conflicting needs and values, and where the teacher or counsellor feels torn in different directions. A line of action which is appropriate for one problem need not necessarily be applied directly to another.

There are various guidelines suggesting situations in which counsellors may have to vary or break client confidences. Here are some of them:

> Information received in confidence is revealed only after the most careful deliberation and when there is clear and imminent danger to an individual or to society, and then only to appropriate professional workers or public authorities. (American Psychological Association (A.P.A.))

> When the client's condition indicates that there is clear and imminent danger to the client or others, the [helper] must take reasonable personal action to inform responsible authorities ... consultation with other professionals must be used where possible. (American Personnel and Guidance Association (A.P.G.A))

In fact, professional codes of ethics offer *broad* guidelines and are often criticised for being too general. Words like duty, values, accountability, confidentiality are used in professional codes of ethics but their precise meaning is often open to debate. They may be interpreted in different ways by different people. Is confidentiality, for example, an absolute concept, or can it be breached in certain circumstances? This is a question which recurs and to which there is no easy answer. But all counsellors need to be aware of the limits of the confidentiality which they offer their clients. As do the clients.

The intention of those who draw up the codes of ethics – usually practitioners themselves – is not for colleagues to adhere blindly to a set of rules of conduct but to thoughtfully and actively engage in a process of ethical reasoning. Nevertheless, the responsibility can be experienced as a heavy burden by counsellors when, sooner or later, they encounter a thorny problem in their work to which there seems to be no right answer and very little hope of a solution. Whose fault is it if things go wrong?

Counsellors treat with confidence personal information about clients, whether obtained directly, or indirectly by inference. Within the school setting, teachers will already have a good deal of information about the client – the pupil – but in other counselling situations, even such basic details as name, address, biographical information, and other descriptions of the client's life and circumstances, which might result in identification of the client, should be regarded as confidential. Whether within the school or any other setting, counsellors' discussion of the clients with professional colleagues should be purposeful and avoid trivialisation (B.A.C., 1984).

Practical issues in education

Much of the literature which deals with ethical issues in counselling is concerned with those situations where the relationship exists as a discrete entity. When a client approaches a counsellor, this is the only relationship they have, and they do not meet outside of the counselling situation. Within schools, however, it is extremely rare to have one adult who works solely as a counsellor. It is more usual to find teachers with pastoral responsibility having to teach, keep discipline *and* be counsellors. One of us has run counselling courses in schools for teachers studying for an M.Ed. degree: an activity on this course is to ask teachers to describe some of the difficulties they perceive in the dual role of teacher/counsellor. The following list comes from the responses of five separate groups of teachers, spanning a three year period. There is a marked similarity of concerns expressed. These concerns are subsumed under three headings: difficulties imposed by *self*; difficulties imposed by the *client* and difficulties relating to the *school*.

Difficulties imposed by *self*:

- unsure how to elicit a response;
- difficulties in relating to some pupils;
- self-confidence;

- saying 'no';
- how I view my role as a teacher;
- problems in making value judgements;
- personality/personal style;
- frustration at giving and not receiving.

Difficulties imposed by the *client*:

- establishing the ground rules;
- confidentiality;
- teachers seen as agents of discipline;
- teachers seen as part of the establishment;
- pupil expectations;
- expectations of other staff;
- pupils sent for counselling.

Difficulties imposed by the *institution*:

- time;
- space;
- timetabling constraints;
- low status of pastoral staff;
- unsympathetic staff.

When working with children there are factors which we need to consider which relate specifically to the adult/child as well as to the client/counsellor relationship. These are alluded to in the responses given above. The main considerations relate to confidence and skills; confidentiality; and role-switching.

Personal qualities and experiences of the counsellor

All schools of counselling recognise the importance of the personal qualities of the counsellor in creating opportunities for change in the client. Most counsellors, too, would agree that the nature of the relationship has a powerful influence on clients' capacity to recognise and understand significant issues in their lives. That relationship is based on trust. Counsellors vary, as we have seen, in the emphasis which they place on the relationship.

Adherents of attachment theory would see the client as working out issues *through* the relationship with the counsellor and so being freed from unresolved past conflicts in order to engage positively with relationships in the present. Rational Emotive Therapy too would consider that trust is essential as a basis for a rational negotiation of action to be taken. Whatever their emphasis, counsellors are in a powerful position in relation to their clients. This in itself poses some serious ethical questions which are particularly relevant when there are difficulties in the relationship, for example when real or imagined abuse of trust occurs.

The counsellor may have deep needs which are being satisfied by the counselling relationship: he or she may unconsciously be meeting his or her own needs rather than those of the client. For example, the counsellor may enjoy the experience of being needed and sabotage attempts on the part of the client to become independent. The counsellor may have difficulties in coping with angry confrontations and so collude with the client in avoiding them; the counsellor may have strong views on what is right or wrong in a relationship which get in the way of helping the client. Working around sexual issues in counselling may cause particular difficulties for a counsellor if the subject evokes unresolved conflicts from the past or difficulties from the present. It is certainly not ethical to use the counselling session as an opportunity to work through your own issues.

Counsellors may be unaware of the impact which insensitivity on their part can have on some clients. For example, one girl described how upsetting it was when a teacher, in an attempt to be helpful, asked her to read aloud a poem describing feelings about death soon after the death of her mother. Insensitive responses by fellow pupils and by teachers ensured that many of her feelings were covered up and a false cheerfulness emerged. Similarly, Mary, now 16, describes her unhappiness when she was being bullied and called nasty names at school because of her disability. 'No one listened. The teachers got tired of my complaints and said I must toughen up. They said I was much too sensitive.' The main ethical issue here is that we cannot quantify how much a person is suffering. Regardless of the behaviour of the client, counsellors have a responsibility to listen and to create a context which will facilitate clients' capacity to work through their difficulties.

It is central to most approaches to counselling that the counsellor be actively engaged in the search for self-knowledge and understanding. To counsellors working in the psychodynamic tradition this involves sensitivity to their own responses to the client: for example, counsellors need to know when a reaction is caused by client emotions and when it is caused by their own unresolved personal conflicts. Counsellors engaged in a rational emotive model need to clarify for themselves that they have accurately helped the client to identify their irrational beliefs. Counsellors also need to protect themselves from burnout, or stress from being exposed over periods of time to the distress of their clients.

It is recommended by some training courses that trainee counsellors undergo their own personal therapy. Others require participation in awareness groups where the opportunity is given for trainees to gain direct experience of being in the role of the client and exploring unconscious processes in the client–therapist relationship. They then reflect on the interactions and the dynamics of the group, the relationships within the group, and the support given to facilitate learning about interpersonal relationships and unconscious processes. Students on many training courses are encouraged to keep a personal journal in which they record their thoughts and feelings about their own personal journey as counsellors.

In order to deal effectively with the ethical issues which counsellors inevitably encounter in their work, it is recommended that they have regular supervision from a qualified counselling supervisor. Within schools, there are some difficulties in that these supportive, supervisory relationships are not usually in existence as a matter of course, and the teacher/counsellor needs to establish them to suit their own particular circumstances and needs. Many teachers who are involved in counselling in schools look towards outside agencies such as the educational psychologist for this supervision. Others form supervisory relationships with colleagues who are also engaged in this type of work.

Values and personal belief systems

Conflicts of values can also lead to ethical dilemmas. Counsellors may unwittingly fail to recognise that their own personal and professional values have a strong influence on their particular stance in therapy. By imposing your own values on clients, you run the risk of diminishing their feelings of self-worth and of increasing the likelihood that they will reject the counselling process. Some clients will turn in despair only to those who share their experiences.

Part of our personal belief system relates to what we consider to be 'normal' or 'healthy'. These beliefs are integral to us and could easily be at odds with what our client is saying. For example, consider the case of one young woman who describes how, when at school, she fell in love with a female teacher, and how the teacher abruptly broke off contact with her. There was no one to talk to about this. 'She told me

I was disturbed and needed help – but she did not say how I could get this help.' Anthony (1982) argues that 'there is no particular therapy for lesbians, but, rather, psychotherapy for women who happen to be lesbians'. (p. 53). An alternative perspective comes from Kitzinger (1987) who is not placated by 'liberal humanists' such as Anthony. She proposes a radical feminist alternative which views lesbianism and heterosexuality as political institutions, neither of which is 'natural'; lesbianism, from this perspective 'poses a threat to patriarchy' and cannot be integrated into the social order.

Another integral aspect of our personal belief system concerns our culture. Because these cultural beliefs are so ingrained and relate to the very essence of our earliest experiences we need to be acutely aware of how people from other cultures may experience and interpret situations. This does not mean that the counsellor/client relationship must be confined to others of the same culture, gender or life experiences, but rather that the counsellor needs to be aware of potential differences and difficulties in their own and their clients' values and belief systems. Let us take, for example, an account by a white counsellor in a sixth-form college. Here, the counsellor is talking about his counselling sessions with an 18-year-old girl:

> She told me she had been coerced into marriage with her cousin while visiting Pakistan, and that she had only given in because the family had threatened not to allow her to return to England unless she complied. Now her father and brothers are beginning to insist that she start making the arrangements to get her husband to England. She was adamant that she did not want him and never had. She said that life at home with her father, her brothers, and their families was unbearable. She even talked about taking an overdose . . .

The counsellor was horrified at what he was hearing and overstepped his role by colluding with his client and encouraging an escape bid which was not practical and not in keeping with her own cultural view of herself. He attempted to give her solutions from a middle-class Western perspective rather than encourage her to devise her own way of dealing with this situation.

Keeping to the contract

Part of the contract inherent in a counselling relationship is the duty of the counsellor to offer the client a competent standard of counselling. This means adequate training, appropriate in-service work, updating of skills and on-going supervision from a qualified counsellor. Counsellors need to continue to work on personal issues throughout their working life. Supervision and personal awareness are a significant part of this process.

It is also important to be aware of the limits of your competence so that you can refer clients on where appropriate. However; even when a client is particularly challenging, sometimes it is in the client's best interest to continue seeing the same counsellor, provided that he or she is having supportive, skilled supervision. Clients too should have access to information about the counsellor's qualifications and experience in the field. With children, this could involve a simple but sensitive explanation of how and why the sessions will be conducted and why you are the person who will be involved.

Other aspects of the contract involve negotiating when to end the relationship and what is permissible within it – for example, how much comforting, touching or holding is mutually acceptable. Since often the counsellor is using the actual relationship to help the client to work through significant personal issues, feelings of loss may well be reactivated as the end of counselling approaches. How this is managed can have a significant impact on the effectiveness of the counselling.

On a more mundane level, arrangements like where the sessions will take place, and when they will start and finish need to be established. These details create a climate of respect for the client and set the relationship on a formal level. All too often teachers comment that they have to squeeze in counselling work with children between their other commitments. As we saw earlier, time and place were two areas of difficulty experienced by teachers. Dealing with this, and getting it right, is a practical ethical issue.

The type of client being treated

The majority of students who will receive counselling in schools are those who are in trouble. This may be because of the ways in which they are behaving or because of difficulties they are having with learning. This means that they are already very vulnerable in terms of the way in which they fit in to the expectations of the system. This is different from the adult client population who usually seek out counselling because of the way they feel – unhappy. Whilst these children and young people may well feel unhappy, their status in terms of power is at an imbalance with the adult teaching population. It may be harder for them to acknowledge their feelings because this would make them more vulnerable. As Sinanson (1993), writing about her experiences of counselling children with learning difficulties, points out:

> censoring the spoken language of hate, anger, despair and envy does not make those issues go away. Rather, it creates disowned, split-off acts of violence. (p. 195)

Roles and responsibilities

Counsellors may find themselves torn between the needs of their client and the constraints of their organisation. They may find themselves involved in the difficult task of prioritising conflicting needs, wants and obligations. In general, counsellors are likely to feel that their client has priority. However, it would be unethical to meet the client's needs if this meant directly and unwillingly being asked to challenge the policies of your own organisation; breaking the law; putting other people at risk; or going counter to your own personal belief system. At the same time, it is essential to make these constraints on the limit of your contract clear to the client. Rarely, however, are these issues clear and where decisions are difficult to reach it is important to seek help for yourself, for example from your supervisor.

Confidentiality

Complaints are often levied towards child and adolescent psychiatric services because of their seeming reluctance to share information about a child or a family. Teachers in particular say that they often feel excluded from treatment and intervention plans, or from information which they might find useful. This is because psychiatry, as a branch of medicine, is bound by the medical ethical code of confidentiality. The arguments for and against this code will not be discussed in any detail here as we wish to concentrate on educational settings. Within schools, the situation is very different. Teachers do share information about pupils and it is usually the case that it would be remiss not to do so. However, when a pupil and teacher engage in a counselling relationship the situation shifts somewhat. The issue of confidentiality emerges, but this is bound with the needs and duties of the teacher/counsellor to share relevant information with colleagues. But how does the teacher/counsellor know where to draw the line? Here, the 'need to know' principle comes into force. Who, amongst teacher colleagues, needs to know what the child or young person has told you? You yourself may well feel overwhelmed or disturbed by what you have heard, and will want to talk to somebody about it. Discussing your own feelings about the counselling work which you are undertaking, or passing on useful and practical information or suggestions to colleagues is a far cry from staff-room gossip, or gratuitously reliving a confidential conversation with colleagues. Once you have established that you are engaging in a counselling relationship with a young person the distinction becomes obvious. However, we all need to be aware of what information we are passing on, how we are doing it and why.

Of course the situation is different once again when the child or young person has given their consent to your discussing their problems with somebody else. You may well decide during your counselling session with Terry that he could best be helped by receiving guidance on science exam revision from the science teacher. If Terry agrees to this you may both agree that you will approach the science teacher on his behalf. However, if during the session, Terry has talked to you in confidence about his relationship with his parents and how they reacted to his poor mark, then you would need to negotiate with Terry as to whether this information should also go to the science teacher. In other words, does the science teacher 'need to know'?

Concluding considerations

For all counsellors there are ethical considerations in relation to the information received from clients and the way in which the counsellor responds to the client's feelings. Appropriate skills, practice and supervision are tools which the counsellor will have acquired and which will guide them through these considerations. In addition, the teacher/counsellor will need to be aware of potential role conflicts when undertaking this sensitive work with vulnerable children.

Whilst Codes of Ethics do exist for counsellors, we suggest that these are guidelines rather than directives. In the final analysis, counsellors must take personal responsibility for their own reactions, behaviour and practices.

CHAPTER SIX

Helping Children to Feel Better About Themselves

The evolving sense of self

The social and emotional development of children is deeply embedded in a sense of self and in the nature and quality of relationships with others, both peers and adults. Much has been written on the subject of the self in the hundred years since William James (1892) identified two distinct but interrelated aspects – the self-as-subject (the 'I') and the self-as-object (the 'me').

The self-as-subject, or the sense of existential identity as more recent writers prefer to call it, emerges as the child develops awareness of self as an entity separate from others, of self as unique and distinctive, and of self as having continuity over time; as the child develops in the capacity to take a reflective stance on the self; and as the child acquires a sense that he or she is actively engaged in understanding and forming experiences and relationships. This is a long process which grows out of the child's earliest interactions with caregivers in the family and which evolves throughout the school years from a complex interweaving of social experience and activity.

The concept of self-as-object refers to the child's capacity to view self as if from the outside, with qualities, attributes, characteristics and abilities. Again, this capacity to take the perspective of other people evolves over time. The process is strongly influenced by the internalised attitudes of other people as the child learns about the range of categories which people use to define the person. As they develop, children learn about gender and other social roles, and about cultural identity; they learn about power and dominance; they learn about liking and being liked, accepting and being accepted.

The internal working model: a concept from attachment theory

As we saw in chapter three, attachment theorists claim that the early experiences of relationships with significant others have long-term implications for the child's future social and emotional development. Children are constantly in a process of negotiating and renegotiating the balance between being attached to others and being independent as they encounter each new developmental phase. Attachment theorists use the concept of the internal working model of relationships. This refers to an internal representation of relationships which exists outside conscious awareness and is rooted in early experience. From this perspective, the internal working model provides a template which influences social behaviour both within and outside the family context. For example, children who have had loving, accepting relationships with parents in the early years will develop different internal working models from those whose attempts to relate to significant adults have been blocked or rejected.

The normal pattern of interaction between child and caregiver is characterised by sensitivity to the child's needs, respect for the child's autonomy, concern to enable the child to develop appropriate independence, and a reliable response to the child's distress. Children who have been cared for in this way build up an internal working model of relationships founded in a secure base. Such children are likely to maintain this pattern with others outside the family circle and to feel secure enough to develop increasingly independent attachments with others. Secure pre-schoolers and five- to seven-year-olds respond positively to a parent on reunion (for example, at the end of the school day) and seem to be able to combine attention to the parent with the capacity to explore their environment and make new friendships. Separation is less stressful to these children than it was when they were babies since they seem to have developed an internal working model which assumes that the parent will be there when needed and which allows for reasonable separation. These children are likely to demonstrate continuity in their pattern of secure attachment to others throughout middle childhood and adolescence.

By contrast, the problem facing the insecurely attached child is the need to maintain attachment with a caregiver who is unpredictable or rejecting. The internal working model here is based on coping with and accommodating to a caregiver who is often 'unavailable', whether physically or emotionally, to meet the child's needs. Avoidant children who have had a harsh experience of relationships, who have been rejected or who have failed to be comforted when distressed, will have low expectations of relationships. They may act in ways which elicit rejection or display a coldness and lack of empathy for others' feelings in their interactions with peers. Anxious-ambivalent children may well remain preoccupied with the relationship with parents, continue to find separation from them distressing at an age when other children are becoming increasingly independent, remain immature and clingy, and be inappropriately demanding in their relationships with peers.

Attachment theorists maintain that the patterns of attachment established in infancy are carried through into childhood and adulthood. However, the internal working model can change in response to concrete experience and, during adolescence, through the process of abstract thinking about self and relationships.

The concept of the internal working model gives us a useful metaphor which gives insight into emotional and social processes in the development of the self and which allows us to conceptualise change through new life experiences, through personal development work on self, or through active intervention by, for example, a teacher or a counsellor.

Beliefs about the self: the rational emotive perspective

Although the terminology differs, rational emotive theorists, like attachment theorists, claim that the person's belief system about the self (another way of conceptualising the internal working model) strongly influences how that individual relates to others and perceives the self. Rational emotive theorists, however, place less emphasis on unconscious processes and early experience than do attachment theorists. Their focus is to a much greater extent on the here-and-now and on the current belief system of the person, wherever that came from. Self esteem is seen as a value judgement about the self which comes between the person's self-image – myself as I am – and the ideal self – myself as I would like to be. The ideal self is that part of the person which strives for personal improvement. When realistic and moderate it is a positive influence. However, people, including children, often make themselves quite unhappy when their ideal is not attainable.

If the person's beliefs about self are positive then self-esteem will be high. A person with high self esteem can accept that they have strengths and failings because they have a fundamental belief in their own self worth. High self esteem is important because it provides a secure base for learning and social development. It facilitates risk-taking, which is necessary to learn new skills and deal with situations and relationships. By contrast, if a negative evaluation is dominant then the self-esteem will be low. Children with low self-esteem are unable to accept that they are worthwhile and are likely to be afraid of making mistakes or failing. Low self-esteem is not always negative and can be an understandable reaction to personal disappointment.

How children feel about themselves

While it is not easy to make direct measurements of an abstract concept such as the self, teachers can learn much from their own observations of children as they interact with one another. In addition, self-descriptions by children at different ages tell us a great deal about the ways in which they see themselves and the ways in which other people's judgements can affect their self-esteem.

The first extensive study of self-esteem in children was made by Coopersmith (1967). He looked at the origins of self-esteem and its continuity over time. His self-esteem inventory was designed to elicit ways in which children saw themselves in relation to peers, parents, school and personal interests. On the basis of this measure, Coopersmith found high correlations between the different areas, and so suggested that it was possible to derive a global or overall estimate of self-esteem.

However, more recently, the validity of a global measure of self-esteem has been challenged. Even although Coopersmith found it to be stable over time (up to three years after the initial testing children's global scores on self-esteem were fairly consistent), psychologists have felt that inventories like Coopersmith's might not be sensitive enough to variations in the child's sense of self-esteem in different areas of their lives. Harter (1985), using a self-perception profile for children, identified five separate domains: scholastic competence; athletic competence; social acceptance; behavioural conduct; physical appearance. Instead of giving children a 'like me/unlike me' choice (as Coopersmith did), Harter offered children four options. Here is an example:

some kids are popular with others their age	BUT	other kids are not very popular
really true of me . . . sort of true of me.		really true of me . . . sort of true of me

For children younger than eight, she devised a picture version showing a competent and a less competent child. The child was asked to choose the picture 'most like me' and then to indicate whether it was 'a lot like me' or 'a little like me'.

Harter's work indicated wide differences in the five domains which she investigated. For example, a child might see herself as highly competent at sport but feel very negatively about her physical appearance. In-depth interviews confirm Harter's findings. Children can feel very positively about themselves in one domain and yet have a deep sense of insecurity in another. Here we look at the self-descriptions given by two children. Nazia, a ten-year-old, describes herself in this way:

> I am in Year 6 at Woodlands Junior School. I have long, black hair which I wear in plaits. I like bright colours like pink and yellow. I'm quite tall for my age. I like the way I look. People say I smile a lot. I'm quite popular. I think that's because I'm helpful and friendly to other people. At least that's what other children say about me. I have two friends, Shabina and Zuleika who are my best friends. We share a lot of secrets with each other. My brother, Afsal, is younger than me and I don't share secrets with him. Sometimes I think he gets his own way too much. But I try not to be angry with him. I do well at school and I feel very proud of that. I'm not quite so good at sports. I really want to be a doctor when I grow up. My mum and dad say that I will really need to study hard to do that. My cousin is studying to be a doctor and he talks to me about his work. Me and my friends are sometimes kept out of games. Rough boys like Sean shout at us – they call us 'Paki' – and tell us to go away.

Sean, aged nine, sees himself in this way.

> I'm very popular and I put it down to my good looks and my personality. Also, I'm clever at sport and I just share things and that. I'm best friends with Ian and Jason. We've been friends for years. We play football a lot at breaktime and after school. We have only good players in our team. We don't let crap players in. There's millions of footballs in t'yard and they know they just want to annoy me 'cos they don't like me saying no to them. Some kids get on my nerves. Like Robert. Wee Robert Mackay. His breath damages ozone layer. I hit him 'cos he gets on my nerves. Every time you tap him he says, 'Stop tickling me!' So I just hit him. I like playing tricks on other people. It is good fun. I put drawing pins on their seats and wiggly worms on their desks. Yes and it's funny. They know I'm going to do it because I tell them I'm going to, and then they start screaming and they get right mad at me.

Nazia shows high self-esteem in the domain of academic competence and behavioural conduct. She is proud of her school work and has academic ambitions for her future studies. She is also developing awareness of when it is appropriate to express feelings such as anger, and when it is less appropriate; this includes some possible resentment in her perception that her brother is treated more indulgently than she is within the family. She feels positively about her capacity to sustain close friendships with Shabina and Zuleika. She is less confident in the playground where domineering aggressive children can easily overrule her.

Sean feels extremely confident about his athletic competence and his physical appearance. He is less realistic about his social acceptance in his peer group since he appears unaware that his aggressive behaviour leads other children to view him with fear rather than genuine friendship. He can command loyalty from his close allies, Ian and Jason, but although he is accepted and valued by them, he is viewed with mixed feelings by the rest of the class.

Academic performance and self-esteem

Hartley (1986) looked at the effects of children's beliefs about themselves on their academic output. He was interested in 'the attribution of competence and the school experience of disadvantaged children'. He devised a situation in which a group of low-achieving children were asked to role-play 'being clever' on a particular task. He found that these children made significantly fewer errors and took significantly longer to think about the questions both during and after the experiment. This study shows the effect that teachers' expectations can have on pupils' self esteem which can, in turn, affect pupil performance.

Wedge and Essen (1982) defined social disadvantage in terms of family composition, poor housing and low income. Children from disadvantaged families had many more difficulties than other children and performed significantly less well at school. However, Wedge and Essen argued that the poor scholastic results of the disadvantaged could be attributed to quite a large extent to the tendency of teachers to enter them for fewer examinations. Even when they scored in the top range on attainment tests, these children were less likely to be entered for examinations in maths and English than others in their year group with similar scores. The teachers seemed to have low expectations about what these pupils could achieve academically.

Studies of the achievement of black pupils (Eggleston 1985; Swann, 1985) showed similar results. A self-fulfilling prophecy seemed to be operating with teachers expecting less of African-Caribbean boys in particular. As one black child quoted in the Swann Report put it:

> In a lot of books you find lovely, pretty pictures, but the pictures are white postmen, white businessmen. You never see a black postman, you never read about black scientists, black whatever. It is always white. If you can't identify yourself with something that you are learning then it is going to kill the incentive in you to learn or go further. (p. 97)

Troyna and Hatcher (1992) provide disturbing evidence that racism plays a significant part in the cultures of predominantly white primary schools. For many black children the experience of racist name-calling is a common one. Even children who seem to be friends can lapse into racist remarks, as Zabeel found:

> Interviewer: So you thought that people had stopped calling you names.
> Z: Yes, then after that I heard people call me names. Like say Mark makes fun, say a Muslim or an Indian can't talk very good he goes '...' (Zabeel put on a mock-Indian accent) and he makes fun and then he goes 'That's a bit like Zab'. I don't want to hit Mark ... He's a good mate. And one day there was this boy Paul and there was these Muslim girls, and the ball went over there and he never knew I was there because if he knew I was there he wouldn't have called them anything, and he said 'Hey you niggers pass me the ball' and when he saw me he goes 'Oh oo, I never said it to you Zab'. (p. 87)

Wright (1992) reviews a number of classroom-based studies which overall paint a disturbing picture. She points out that the evidence indicates a situation in schools where it is commonplace that teachers are 'meting out different treatment to more or less favoured groups of pupils' (p. 15). Wright's own observations in four inner city primary schools confirmed distinct differences in the ways white teachers treat black children. Here she describes what she saw during typical class discussion sessions in one nursery school:

> In these formal sessions, the Asian children were generally observed to be excluded from the discussion because of the assumption that they could not understand or speak English. On the occasions when the Asian children were encouraged to participate in a group discussion, teachers often communicated with them using basic telegraphic language. When this strategy failed to get any responses the teachers would quickly lose patience with the chldren and would then ignore them. (p. 16)

Wright observes that the cumulative effect of teachers' attitudes towards Asian children was 'to create a sense of insecurity for these children in the classroom' (p. 19). This in turn had an effect on their peer relationships.

> They were extremely unpopular, especially among their white peers [who would] use aspects of the exchanges between the teacher and the Asian child that referred to perceived personal deficiencies to tease and taunt their Asian classmates. (p. 19)

According to Wright, the Afro-Caribbean child has a different, but no less distressing experience.

> Essentially, it was observed that whenever Afro-Caribbean children were present they were always amongst the most criticised and reprimanded children in the group. Moreover, there was a greater willingness for some teachers to reprimand Afro-Caribbean children (especially boys) for similar behaviour ignored when adopted by other children. (p. 19)

It is important that schools create the kind of social climate where racist behaviour is consistently challenged, where positive interpersonal relationships are valued and where there is a supportive atmosphere which is conducive for all pupils to learn to work together. Cowie, Smith, Boulton and Laver (1994) have shown the positive impact which a co-operative group-work curriculum can have on the enhancement of relationships in the multi-ethnic classroom, but also the difficulties which can be encountered, especially when the classrooms contain significant numbers of disruptive pupils.

Maxime' (1993) reviews evidence that some black children in Britain hold extremely negative views of 'blackness' in self and others. These children have 'a very poor racial concept of self and often claim to hate themselves' (p. 100). In her view, this identity/confusion requires therapeutic help for the individual child. In addition, she has developed workbooks (Maxime', 1991) to be used in the classroom with children aged between seven and twelve years which can help them enhance their own sense of racial identity and intervene to halt the development of self-hatred.

The process is, of course, two way. Pupils do not always receive the same message that the teacher is trying to give. A child may not recognise praise, or may not accept or believe praise if it does not fit in with their own belief system about themselves. It is very difficult if not almost impossible for the teacher to get the balance of praise exactly right for every pupil in the class, in a similar way that it is difficult to attune the curriculum to every pupil's ability and interest level. A pupil with poor self-esteem can engender feelings of frustration and

Figure 4: THE SPIRAL OF SELF-ESTEEM

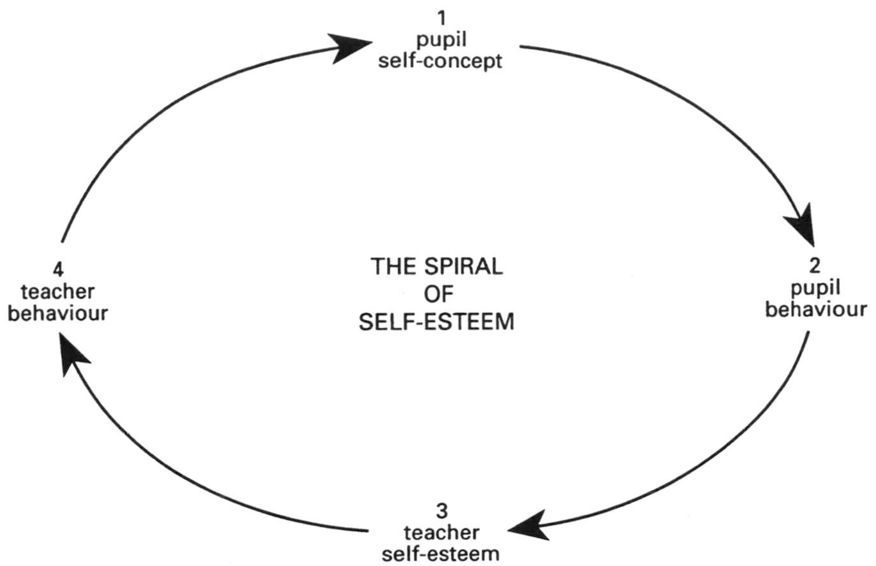

anger within the teacher. They often appear not to try, to be attention seeking or fail to respond to the teacher's best endeavours. We all know that children pick up on such reactions so that a cycle of continuing negative self-esteem is engendered (see figure 4).

The impact of abuse on self-esteem

Abuse of young people may be physical, sexual or emotional. It may stem from home, from the community, from peers or from school. The more extreme forms of abuse are, thankfully, rare. Most adults do not wish to abuse or harm children, but many adults do so unintentionally. For example, punishment of children is a part of every family's culture and usually families get the balance more or less right. It is all too easy to 'blame' families for imbuing their child with a poor self-image. The intention, for example, behind a mother berating her child for not learning her spellings may be benign and supportive. Sometimes, however, the punishment is inappropriate to the child's needs, and the message received by the child may be unnecessarily negative, particularly if the family tends to have a harsh, critical ethos. The child may then internalise a low sense of self-esteem.

Any form of abuse, no matter how mild, will affect the young person's view of self. Research shows (see examples in Corby 1993) that children who have been abused suffer from an excess of self-criticism which, over a period of time, can only lead to poor self-esteem. Although evidence about the consequences of abuse is inconclusive (De Francis 1969; Gomes-Schwartz et al. 1990), the behavioural manifestations range from the well-hidden and carefully disguised to hyperactivitity and the inability to settle for any substantial length of time to a task. In addition, behaviour can include 'frozen watchfulness' and 'frozen aggression', responses which describe a suspicion and wariness of other people, usually adults. This is the phenomenon seen in those children who seem to wish to hurt others for no identifiable reason. Someone who feels good about themselves does not need to do this.

This has implications for the school's system of punishment. Hurting others is usually followed by some form of punishment, if detected. But teachers are in the difficult situation of having to balance the institution's need for maintaining discipline following harm to another on the one hand with the desire to meet the needs of (if not fully understand) the aggressor on the other. Very few other professional workers have to face this dilemma.

Take the example of bullying. The rational emotive theorist considers the actors in a bullying scenario in terms of their self-esteem. The players are the bully, the victim(s) and the bystanders. In terms of the way in which they perceive themselves, both the bully and the victim clearly have difficulties with their self-image. Both behaviours are extremes of a self-defeating continuum. We can argue that both are demonstrating low self-esteem, although this may not be the case, and it could be that the bully is maintaining a misplaced sense of high self-esteem. The bystanders on the other hand are a mixture of bully and victim. It has been demonstrated that bullying has significant effects on those who watch but are not active participants. The confusion and impotence which they felt had the effect of lowering their own self-esteem. This demonstrates the fact that one does not have to be active or instrumentally passive to have one's self-esteem affected.

As we saw, attachment theory argues that the child develops an internal working model of relationships that may be secure or insecure (avoidant, ambivalent or disorganised). Unless there are changes in life circumstances (or an internal re-evaluation that is unlikely to happen before adolescence) these patterns will show continuity into relationships throughout the school years. One study has made a specific link to bully–victim relationships. Troy and Sroufe (1987) characterised 38 children according to the attachment relationship they had with their mothers. When the children were four to five years old, they were assigned to same-gender playgroups. All cases of bullying occurred when a child with an avoidant attachment history (the bully) was paired with a child with an anxious attachment history (the victim). Children who were securely attached were able to detach themselves from bullying or being bullied. Turner (1991) found that insecurely attached boys showed more aggressive and controlling behaviours towards peers. What this may mean is that children with avoidant-insecure attachment relationships lack trust and expect hostility and so may develop aggressive patterns of relationships with peers. By contrast, children with ambivalent-insecure relationships with parents are likely to be receiving unpredictable care, so they have to expend a lot of energy in trying to get the attention they need. They stay dependent and also lack self-esteem and confidence in themselves. They are thus more vulnerable to being bullied by peers. This model places more emphasis on the child's internal working model of relationships than on the child's repertoire of social skills. However, there is clearly strong evidence to support the view that by teaching these children – bullies and victims – a different repertoire of social skills and by enlisting the support of bystanders, peer relationships can be changed for the better (see Smith, Bowers, Binney and Cowie, 1993).

Promoting self-esteem

Positive self-esteem is vital to achievement, both in work and in relationships. Manifestations of either passive or active low self-esteem are not useful for the individual child or for the harmonious functioning of the classroom. Children with low self-esteem are hard on themselves and hard on their teachers. In particular, children with learning difficulties can easily see themselves as failures, which further hampers their learning and their development. Something which we can all too easily forget is that learning requires confidence.

As can be imagined, schools and teachers are highly significant in terms of the self-image which a child creates and maintains for themselves. The school ethos, management structure and day-to-day routines should be focussed to enhance children's self-image. This is done

Figure 5: PASSIVE AND ACTIVE DEMONSTRATIONS OF LOW SELF-ESTEEM

Passive	Active
not participating	attention seeking
quiet	spoiling others' work
avoiding new situations	spoiling own work
afraid of failure	putting others down
easily giving up	easily provoked
easily threatened	aggressive
dependent on others	rejecting of others

through systems and procedures which make children feel valued, both at an institutional (school) level and at an individual (teacher and peer) level. Most children incorporate these positive elements into their self-concept. However, there are some children who do not inculcate these positive approaches into their feelings about themselves. They demonstrate, in various ways, a low or poor self-image, and their behaviour demonstrates a lack of personal valuing. The within-school or within-class reward and positive reinforcement systems in place do not touch these children. They are unhappy. It is true to surmise that the largest proportion of children who are referred for counselling help are children with poor self-esteem. These children demonstrate their negative feelings about themselves in various ways according to age, temperament, previous experiences, intelligence and habit. Figure 5 lists some of these.

Counselling for self-esteem

Most children acquire a realistic view of themselves with appropriate levels of self valuing and critical appraisal. Some, however, as we have seen, because of their experiences, fail to appreciate their own strengths and weaknesses and relate to other people in ways which maintain their negative opinions about themselves. Their low self-esteem may only be inferred by teachers through, for example, unacceptably aggressive behaviour, isolation or poor attainment. As we saw in chapter two, counselling children with low self-esteem is only one way of supporting them. It is possible to enhance self-esteem within the classroom by such methods as cooperative group work, through the personal and social education curriculum and through a whole school policy on the community values of the school. There are various texts (Gurney, 1986;

Robinson and Maines, 1988) and courses on enhancing the self-esteem of children within the classroom. However, for some children, there may come the point when it is necessary to offer them individual counselling.

In the following sections we look at strategies, based on attachment theory and on rational emotive theory, which the counsellor might use to help children whose low sense of self-esteem is preventing them from forming positive relationships with others and from realising their academic potential.

Facilitating change in the pupil's internal working model

As we saw earlier in this chapter, the child's internal working model, based on experiences within the family, may cause difficulties in forming relationships with peers and teachers. Coping strategies which served a purpose in the past (perhaps as a means of protecting the self from emotional distress) become increasingly inappropriate in the present and, in extremes, may create a false knowledge of other people. For example, in chapter three, Lesley's experience of her parents seems to have been that they were cold and rejecting. Because of hospitalisation, Lesley was separated from her mother and bonding was difficult at that stage in her life. Since her needs were not always met, Lesley developed an internal working model of significant adults as being absent and uncaring. Later she applied this model of relationships to other authority figures like teachers. By perceiving her teachers in this way and interacting with them as if they were bound to reject her she confirmed this pattern of relating to others. To protect herself against this expected rejection Lesley often appeared surly and was unlikely to show a friendly response when teachers were kind to her. With peers she had similar difficulties in forming warm relationships; with younger or vulnerable children she could act out harsh behaviour patterns through bullying and seldom showed any remorse for what she had done or much empathy for their suffering.

Through the on-going relationship with her counsellor, the deputy head, Mrs Pitt, Lesley discovered the possibility of change. Mrs Pitt offered her a safe haven in which to examine her ways of seeing herself and her model of interacting with other people. Here she was able to explore the feelings of rejection by her parents and to relive the feelings of loss which she had experienced as a younger child when she was 'not lovable like Marie' or when her family found it hard to express warmth and affection. As a child Lesley had learned to hide her tears as they only led to further rejection. She had entered into a pattern of seeming not to care about the losses and separations which happen to all children at points in their lives. When friendships did not last, she could not grieve or bear the risk that others might jeer at her for having hurt feelings. Just as no one had seemed to care for her when she was hurt, so she was unable to show empathy for the children whom she bullied.

Lesley's veneer of surliness was gently challenged by Mrs Pitt and, when the tears finally came, she was enabled to grieve for the closeness which had been lacking in her early life. This sorrow was accepted non-judgementally by Mrs Pitt who gave her time and space to express it. She felt that Lesley was now ready to consider the positive aspects of herself side by side with those aspects which she found unworthy and hateful. This helped Lesley to accept rather than reject the hurt child in herself. She helped Lesley to question and challenge the view that she was unlovable and begin the long process of integration.

As these changes took place in Lesley's understanding of herself, Mrs Pitt helped her to apply the same principles to her current relationships at home and at school. She began to accept that her parents had difficulty in expressing their feelings but that this did not mean that they did not care for her. She began to learn new ways of relating to her peers. Lesley was not skilled at forming relationships with other people so the changes were not easy to make. But the counselling sessions gave her the confidence to build on her new-found inner resources to form a friendship with a girl of her own age. This time, instead of experiencing the everyday ups and downs of a relationship as a rejection Lesley entered the friendship with the expectation that she was worthy of acceptance. She was more tolerant and found that she was able to give more to the relationship. Instead of finding that closeness inevitably leads to pain and rejection Lesley had begun to re-create her internal working model and actively play a part in making some new choices about how she related to other people.

Her counsellor had helped her to understand the links between past and present and, by offering the love and support which she had never been sure of within her own family, helped her to work through her own pain and so to re-create her working model of self and others.

Facilitating change through Rational Emotive Therapy

Let us take another example. Lorraine, like Lesley, was very unhappy because she saw herself as not having any friends. Her counsellor, Mr

Figure 6: *AN A-B-C ANALYSIS*

A – ACTIVATING EVENT	**C – CONSEQUENCES**
Ken and Sarah didn't ask me to be in their group in the drama lesson.	I feel hurt and disappointed.

B – BELIEFS (IRRATIONAL)

1. They should have asked me.
2. I must always be chosen by other people.
3. I ought to be popular and in demand.
4. I can't bear to be left out.
5. I can't stand it.

Davies, who was her form teacher, following an R.E.T. model, started from the point of believing what Lorraine was saying about the way she saw things. Although Mr Davies had observed that she did in fact have friends, he accepted that Lorraine's perception of herself was true to her at that time. He considered too that she might even be behaving in a way so as to distance herself from other people, a pattern which was highly likely in view of her poor image of herself as a friend: 'If people believe things to be real, they are real in their consequences' (Herbert, 1988). Lorraine was making demands on herself and on other people. Through sensitive discussion with Mr Davies the A-B-C analysis emerged. It looked as shown in figure 6.

Lorraine's self-esteem was low because of the interpretation she put on to unpleasant life events. This was her reality. She had held this view for a long time and was resistant to change. This being the case, much patience and time was needed. However, Lorraine's negative reactions to specific situations gave Mr Davies the opportunity to help her to take on board an alternative perspective.

In counselling, he worked towards helping Lorraine to recognise what she was saying to herself and encouraging her, within the safety and security of the counselling session, to challenge the irrationality of her self-talk and to dispute these self-defeating statements. She was then able to evaluate herself in a more positive light which helped her to accept the unpleasant reality of not being everybody's first choice as a partner. At that point, Lorraine was saying to herself that these conditions were intolerable and that she could not bear them to continue. Mr Davies pointed out that of course she was sad, but she could bear it since, as he put it, 'nobody ever died from not being chosen as a partner'.

Mr Davies helped Lorraine to dispute her Irrational Beliefs by

Figure 7: LORRAINE'S RATIONAL BELIEFS

BELIEFS (RATIONAL)
1. It is unpleasant not to be chosen.
2. Being left out is uncomfortable but not unbearable.
3. It would be better if more people asked me to be their partner.

reflecting back her own self-defeating statements, helping her to elaborate on them and thereby to recognise what she was saying to herself. He challenged her 'musts, oughts and shoulds'. Lorraine's more rational beliefs are shown in figure 7.

Mr Davies might have judged that Lorraine sometimes behaved in a way that discouraged others from wanting to be with her. But his view was that this was a separate issue. He chose to deal with it outside the counselling contract. In fact, he suggested to her drama teacher that lessons on making friends might be useful. He might on the other hand have judged that her social behaviour was in fact so awful that what she required was social skills advice rather than counselling. As we emphasise throughout this book, counselling is only one of many options.

Conclusions

Schools exist not only for children, but also for teachers. Our performance at work and the reactions – both real and perceived – which we get from colleagues affect us as adults. It is to be hoped that as intelligent adults we are more able than children and young people to rationalise and make sense of our own performance and feedback. If this were only true then grown-ups would never have any debilitating self-doubts and would never be unhappy. As it is, there are times in our personal and in our professional lives when we have feelings of failure and lack of appreciation. This in turn reduces our own self esteem and our own effectiveness. We need to look after ourselves, to value the support systems which we have available and to acknowledge that we need recognition and praise. An effective pastoral system (see chapter two) will take this into account.

An important fact for teachers to recognise is that they will not be successful with every child they teach. Some, despite the teachers' best endeavours, will fail academically. Others will not alter their behaviour despite the most consistent and scientifically applied principles. Others will continue to reinforce their negative self-image despite the fact that the teacher is both aware and supportive of this possibility. This does not make you a bad teacher even though, at the end of a difficult day some Irrational Beliefs may creep into your self-concept.

The current climate of harsh law enforcement strategies can be seen as a reaction against the 'understanding criminals and wrong-doers' approach of the past two decades. It is no longer 'fashionable' to talk of anti-social acts such as drug-taking or aggression as evidence of psychological disturbance and therefore excusable. Whether or not anti-social acts are excusable under any circumstances is open to debate. However, when dealing with and talking about children and young people we must fall between one of two assumptions. The first assumption is that some people are born plain wicked and/or weak. The second assumption is that whenever a young person 'goes wrong' it is always somebody else's fault. Whilst not wanting to promote this debate, we do wish to suggest that a view somewhere in the middle, moderated and mediated to the needs and circumstances of each child, is most appropriate. For example, there may be many reasons why a young person engages in delinquent behaviour such as drug-taking. Herbert (1988) points out that the key factor in drug-taking is availability. However, this is tempered with other factors such as: encouragement by others; rebelliousness; lack of aspirations, hopes or desires; and poor self-esteem. The lack of self-esteem is paramount in this, as in many other incidents of lawlessness or anti-social behaviour. If so-called anti-social behaviour is a rational choice on the part of the young person then reactions on the lines of punishment or rehabilitation are suggested. If, however (and this is more likely to be the case) the behaviours are the result of negative feelings about his or herself – feelings of powerlessness, of lack of opportunities and lack of optimism – then we need to think in terms of improving the young person's perceptions of self.

As we have seen, self-esteem is generated and maintained through a circular process involving our own behaviours and attitudes and the reactions of others towards these. In addition, our self-esteem makes evaluations about other people's reactions based on what we think of ourselves – our self-concept. The consequence of this on forming and enjoying relationships is complex. If we like ourselves we will be open to positive feedback from others. If we don't like ourselves – our self-esteem is low – then we may either reject as untrue any positive responses from others, or be so desperate for them that we behave in such a way as to discourage other people from getting too close. If we go back to the case of Lorraine, and assume that she usually has high self-esteem, then the rejection she suffered will not in itself alter this. It may make her question herself in a way which is unfamiliar and uncomfortable, but she will be able to accept this without feeling emotionally damaged. On the other hand, her self-esteem may be so low that she expects rejection from others and behaves in a demanding or aggressive way which is off-putting for her peers. The consequence of poor self-esteem on relationships is that, because the individual is not easy to be with, the negative cycle is maintained.

Earlier in this chapter we looked at some studies which demonstrated how a pupil's self-esteem affects learning. Lawrence (1973) demonstrated this graphically in terms of children's reading. He asked the question 'Will he read better if we help him to feel better about himself?' This is the reverse of the question which we usually ask – 'Will she feel better about herself if we teach her to read?' His basic premise was that enhanced self-esteem will affect progress with reading to a greater extent than would extra help. He used volunteer counsellors to work with a group of children who were failing with reading. Lawrence's supposition was found to be correct – helping children to feel better about themselves lead to an increase in academic success.

Some difficult pupils have high self-esteem and may even become folk heroes in their own community. The values of the families may well run counter to the values of the school – for example being strict and punitive, or even violent, while the school is attempting to be 'child-centred', or vice versa. Yet the parents or the teachers may well view themselves as good enough according to their philosophy of child-rearing.

At times, giving extra help to a child who is already failing can be interpreted as a confirmation of that failure. In reality, most schools endeavour to give children with special educational needs a combination of extra help and at the same time take account of their self-image. The two do not have to be mutually exclusive.

CHAPTER SEVEN:

The Abuse of Power

Introduction

Escalations in levels of violence over the last decade illustrate the role which societal events play in the everyday experience of many children. Counselling alone cannot resolve this social problem but it can play a significant part in alleviating personal distress. We cannot ignore the social context within which individual abuse of power takes place. In order to understand the risks to children and young people, we need to consider the integration of a range of factors:

individual/temperamental characteristics: a child may be shy or withdrawn; or may have a disability; the child may be small for his or her age;
the situation: a child may have been labelled by peers as the class victim and be regularly ostracised or ignored; the child may be experiencing prejudice on the basis of being racially or ethnically different from peers;
home circumstances: the child may be living in conditions of material deprivation and poverty; the family may be experiencing emotional stress; the child's parents may be unable or unwilling to provide support;
the peer culture: there may be peer group norms which place high value on displays of aggression and violence;
the community: there may be community attitudes and values which perpetuate discrimination and prejudice against certain groups.

As we saw in chapter two, the Elton Report (DES, 1989) made a strong case for the valuing in schools of supportive interpersonal relationships and a sense of citizenship amongst the pupils. Yet for this to develop well, it is helpful if the school has an active commitment to a policy on children's rights, equality of opportunity and anti-racism in which all members of the school community are involved. The reality is that much of educational practice ignores young people's democratic rights. Few schools actually offer pupils opportunities to be involved in activities where they have scope to be involved in the process of coming to decisions about rules and guidelines for conduct in their own school setting.

In this chapter we look at specific strategies, each rooted in a counselling approach, which have been developed within school contexts to address the issue of the abuse of power. None of these methods is punitive and each gives children the opportunity to develop their interpersonal skills and their capacity to take the perspective of others into account. Children who experience non-punitive, child-centred methods, or who see them being practised by others, are given a chance to respond to difficulties in relating to others which are assertive rather than aggressive and which demonstrate a democratic respectful way of relating to others. The approach which we describe here demonstrates that the resolution of difficulties around the abuse of power need not have winners and losers, but rather that open, honest dialogue can result in outcomes which are in the end beneficial to all who are involved.

School bullying

Bullying in school is a widespread phenomenon experienced by pupils from all backgrounds and in all different kinds of school (Whitney and Smith, 1993; Smith and Sharp, 1994). Yet, in general, fewer than half of pupils who reported being bullied on an anonymous questionnaire had told a teacher or anyone at home about this:

> Jonathon is often involved in fights. He is small in stature and usually comes out the worse for wear. Despite this, he persists in trying to push into the football games of Jason and Darren, dominant boys who shout at him to go away. If he does not go away, they push and kick him. Occasionally they tolerate his presence so he hangs around on the edge of their gang. Wayne is also bullied by Jason and Darren, but at other times he picks on other children without mercy. Jamie and Delroy are onlookers. They turn away and say, 'That's Jonathon getting in another fight again. He asked for it this time' or 'Why doesn't Wayne pick on someone his own size?'
>
> Kamran is a newcomer to the class. He is smartly dressed and his parents give him extra pocket money to spend on the way home. He has not made any friends yet and is usually alone. Jason and Darren regularly go up to Kamran at break in a threatening way and say, 'Come on,

> Paki, give us 50p!' Kamran usually gives them the money, but recently they have started to demand more.

In this example, we see different ways in which children can be involved in bullying. Aggressive victims include children who in some way provoke bullying reactions in their peers, either deliberately or inadvertently through their irritating or inappropriate behaviour, as Jonathon does. They often respond to others in an aggressive way. If unchallenged, they will continue to act like this. Passive victims are regular targets though they do nothing to provoke an attack. They are likely to become fearful, withdrawn or isolated if this happens over a long period of time. Kamran is at risk in this way unless steps are taken to alter the situation. Bully-victims are those children, like Wayne, who are both victimised by others and involved in bullying weaker children. The more that children are bullied, the more they lose their self-esteem. The onlookers, like Delroy and Jamie, are also at risk since, by their failure to challenge the behaviour of Darren and Jason, they are colluding with a situation which they do not like but which they do not know how to stop.

The issue of gender is relevant in any discussion of the abuse of power. Sharp and Smith (1994) point out that boys are predominantly over-represented in samples of pupils who are the victims of bullying behaviour. Girls who are the victims of bullying may be overlooked because bullying amongst girls is more likely to be indirect (for example, name calling or exclusion from games) and therefore less easy to detect. Perhaps the role of passive victim, too, is more likely to be seen as 'normal' for girls and therefore acceptable. In one study (Arora, 1991) teachers nominated significantly more boys than girls for inclusion in a support group for victims. But this does not mean that fewer girls are being victimised.

In the following sections, we look at two strategies which can play a part in combatting bullying behaviour. Each involves an element of group work; each teaches children involved in bullying a specific range of skills; each has been successfully tried out in schools; each is rooted in a counselling approach. We look at assertiveness training which specifically targets vulnerable children and gives them the opportunity to learn empowering skills in the safety of a supportive, trusting group. Next we look at two similar methods – the method of shared concern and the no-blame approach in which an adult counsellor challenges the norms of a bullying group and makes contracts with each member of the gang – and with the victim – to change their behaviour. It is essential for their full effectiveness that the intervention takes place in the context of a whole-school policy. This would normally be a written document which should say what is meant by bullying and clarify the sanctions which will be taken when bullying takes place. Ideally it should involve widespread consultation with all members of the school community, including teachers, parents, lunchtime supervisors and pupils.

Assertiveness training for children who are being bullied

Assertiveness refers to the ability to stand up for one's rights and to express thoughts, feelings and emotions in a clear and honest way which does not abuse other people's rights. Through assertiveness training, pupils can be taught skills such as: making assertive statements; resisting manipulative behaviour; responding to name-calling; getting help from others when appropriate; feeling positively about themselves; remaining calm.

In the following example, we see how a pupil can be trained to deal with a threatening situation.

> Mary moves threateningly towards Rema. She demands that Rema give her maths homework to her. If Rema refuses, she says she will get her after school. Rema stands still, looking Mary directly in the eye. She feels nervous inside but remembers the words which she has rehearsed in her group. She says, 'I don't lend my books.' Mary grabs her arm. Rema repeats her statement again. She does this three times, looking constantly straight into Mary's eyes. Mary walks off empty-handed.

Mary would have persisted in her aggressive behaviour if Rema had cringed or adopted submissive body language. The techniques are effective yet non-violent. Arora (1989, 1991) has taught vulnerable pupils how to avoid being bullied and how to deal with bullying when it occurs. Arora found that after only twelve hours of assertiveness training in groups most pupils' self-esteem had increased. Teachers confirmed this improvement. The pupils themselves reported that there was a decrease in the extent to which they were bullied. Typical pupils' statements about themselves following assertiveness training indicated an increase in confidence:

> I felt I could look them in the eye though I was crying inside.
> I found that people were helpful and kind after all; you only had to ask.

Even after two terms and without follow-up training, pupils were still feeling confident and levels of bullying had fallen. Typically, friendships developed within the assertiveness groups, enabling the pupils to form a network of support. The method is also effective for helping children with special needs who can be especially vulnerable to bullying.

The method of shared concern

In this section and the next, we look at two very similar methods. The first – the method of shared concern – was pioneered in Sweden by Anatol Pikas (1989); the second – the No-blame Approach – was developed by Maines and Robinson (1991) in the UK. Although the procedures in each are slightly different, they share a common commitment to a non-punitive method which is both co-operative and challenging.

Pikas does not deny that there are occasions when bullying takes place between a single bully and another individual or group of individuals, but, he argues, the most common form that bullying in school takes is that of mobbing – a form of group violence where a gang of bullies attack an individual or group either physically or psychologically over a period of time. The group of bullies includes the leaders, their hangers-on and the regular on-lookers who do nothing to protect the victim. As a group, they are caught up in a collective phenomenon – aggression towards a victim. But within the group there will be a range of individual anxieties and reservations about what is happening. For example, some will conform through fear that if they do not, they in turn will become victims. Through peer pressure to conform and through fear of standing out, members of the group will actively participate in bullying or passively collude in it. The counsellor's task is to bring into conscious awareness the feelings of unease or shame which individual group members have about the group's bullying behaviour. Through a series of individual talks with each member of the group, the counsellor establishes an area of common concern about the situation of the victim. The counsellor's task is not to assign blame or to be punitive, but simply to establish agreement that the situation of the victim is not good. The counsellor's understanding of the group's dynamics is combined with initiative and persistence to bring about change, however small, in each member of the group.

Through the first step of establishing an area of common concern the teacher offers the possibility of an escape from the unpleasantness of taking part in the tormenting of a fellow pupil. How is this done?

Each pupil who bullies is invited to take part in devising a constructive solution to the problem. Each suggestion is considered seriously: the teacher discusses, with each member of the bullying group in turn, a realistic way of putting it into practice.

> Farana, aged 9, had been so cruelly punched and teased by Tom and Jason that she was absent from school more often than she attended. Her peers knew what was going on but did nothing to stop it. Usually she was left on her own. No one ever played with her at breaktime. Members of staff had tried every strategy they knew to break the pattern but the difficulty was that most pupils seemed to accept that this was 'normal' treatment for Farana. The deputy head was eager to break this cycle of bullying and decided to try the method of shared concern since, despite frequent appeals to the better nature of Farana's peer-group, nothing seemed to change the situation.

Here are selected extracts from the deputy head's records of the first and last interviews.

> Jason was seen first. He admitted that Farana was feeling bad so very quickly I established this as 'an area of shared concern'. When he was asked, 'What can we do?' he answered that he could leave Farana alone during the next week.

> Tom responded differently. It was hard to make eye contact and he denied any involvement in the bullying of Farana but he did admit that 'other people' called her 'Paki'. He seemed to find this funny. It took a longer time to establish an area of shared concern since he appeared to be totally indifferent to Farana's feelings. However, eventually he agreed to the contract that he would say to the others, 'Stop calling Farana names!' whenever it occurred.

> Farana entered the room last; she was small in stature, very downcast with a dejected posture. It was hard to make eye contact as she kept looking at the floor. She said that Jason used to punch her a lot but that it was much better now since he and Tom 'only called her names'. When we explored this further, she admitted that they called her 'Paki'. She disclosed this information in a very quiet voice. Her face expressed pain but also relief that someone could listen to her story. Her gaze was intent and prolonged. When I proposed the idea of a group meeting she said cautiously that she would rather wait to see how things worked out.

This procedure is repeated at weekly intervals until the counsellor feels that it is time to arrange the group meeting where bullies and victim meet face-to-face to review the situation. It should be stressed that this group meeting would only take place when the victim has stated his or her readiness to meet the group of bullies in this way. The success of this meeting depends very much on how well the counsellor has prepared for it in advance. It is likely that there will be emotional accusations and recriminations on both sides and that the session will take time. However, the counsellor's prime aim is to promote communication amongst all the participants and to facilitate this through positive responses to all the constructive suggestions which emerge.

> I went to the class to collect Tom and Jason. I made sure I praised the two boys for the fact that they had been able to leave Farana alone. We talked in general about the fact that it can be hard to keep to a bargain. No one is perfect. When Farana came in she said quietly to the others that she felt much happier. They looked pleased at this. I said that I would arrange a further meeting at the beginning of term to see how things were going and said again how pleased I was with the outcome of the meetings. The three seemed reluctant to go as they were enjoying this opportunity to talk.
>
> Farana has not been bullied since and has made friends with two other girls who are her constant companions in the playground.

Since the method of shared concern goes through a precise sequence of stages, it is essential to be trained before using it. (For a step-by-step account see Sharp and Smith, 1994.) In addition, it is appropriate to form a support group to share experiences and build up a body of expertise. On the basis of teacher and pupil perceptions, it appears that it can be a powerful tool for combatting bullying in a remarkably short space of time.

The no-blame approach

Maines and Robinson (1991) similarly take the view that the counsellor needs to foster co-operative values such as empathy, concern for others and unselfishness within the group, in the belief that the pupil engaged in bullying behaviour will relinquish power as a result of peer pressure. Maines and Robinson are critical of punitive measures which, in their view, only reinforce the values of hierarchy and dominance through power. They share with Pikas a belief that bullying is a group phenomenon – mobbing – which thrives in a particular kind of peer group culture, and aim to establish an area of shared concern between the group of bullies and their victim. The counsellor starts by talking to the victim about his or her feelings. Next the counsellor arranges to speak with the whole group of pupils who have been involved, including active bullies, hangers-on, bystanders and those who collude. The counsellor tells the group how the victim is feeling and may use a poem, a piece of writing or a drawing to heighten the impact of this account. At no point is blame attributed: rather, the group is encouraged to suggest ways in which the victim could be helped to feel happier. The risk is that some members of this group will remain indifferent to the plight of the victim. But they are so convinced of the power of the peer group itself to facilitate change that the risk is worth taking. The group meeting ends when the counsellor passes over the responsibility for solving the problem to the group. Follow-up interviews a week later with each member of the group ensure continuing involvement on the part of all the young people and an opportunity for the counsellor to monitor progress.

Maines and Robinson recommend that the counsellor take the risk of letting victims speak in their own words of their suffering. In their experience, the impact of the adult listening and then speaking on behalf of the victim is very powerful. They assume that empathy with the victim's hurt will occur if the victim's case is put forcefully by the adult. This counselling approach derives from a basic skill – that of reflecting back to the members of the group what the outcomes of their bullying behaviour are. Empathy occurs, they argue, when group members are reminded of similar experiences of rejection, intimidation or fear in their own lives. It is this capacity for empathy which enables us to take the perspective of another person and to see things from that person's point of view. The no-blame approach builds on this fundamental human capacity.

The evidence that the no-blame approach works is derived from case study material. The video and accompanying workbook (Maines and Robinson, 1992) introduce teachers and pupils to a seven-point plan which aims to enhance feelings of concern for the victim and create the social context in which bullies, victims and bystanders can be engaged in a problem-solving approach. Inside perspectives from all the people involved give greater insights and the no-blame approach offers a useful practical method to add to the counsellor's repertoire of techniques for combatting bullying.

Peer counselling

Although peer influence is often looked upon in a negative way, which requires adults to monitor and control, as teachers and counsellors we can harness it to make a valuable contribution to the creation of a caring environment in school. Peer counselling has the potential to build on children's ability to assist other children who are experiencing personal difficulties at school and to challenge those who abuse their power over others. Carr (1981) defines peer counselling as 'a way for students to learn how to care about others and put their caring into practice'.

Peer counselling is based on evidence that peers may be perceived as being more understanding and approachable than adults. As we saw earlier in this chapter, many victims stay silent about their experiences and so enable the bullies to maintain their aggressive behaviour patterns unchallenged. Typically, in peer counselling programmes, pupils are selected through a carefully planned interview procedure: those who are not deemed to be ready for the role of counsellor can usually be offered administrative work as receptionists. Peer counsellors are given training in basic counselling and support skills, notably active listening, reflecting back, paraphrasing and summarising. Guidance and supervision provide on-going support. In this way, the pupils learn how to be good listeners, to refrain from interrupting, to reflect back and paraphrase what their clients are saying. Emphasis is also placed on the need to be comfortable with silence and emotion. Pupils are taught about body language and social distancing and are observed, during training, as they practise their skills on one another.

The work of Carr (1988), and Sharp, Sellars and Cowie (1994) shows that pupil counsellors are able to offer unique perspectives on why their peers may be suffering socially and personally, and can often identify appropriate strategies for helping them, such as listening sympathetically, understanding that they do not always want to tell a teacher and empowering them to affirm for themselves the action which they should take. Sharp, Sellars and Cowie (1994) evaluated the effectiveness of a peer counselling service in one comprehensive school. Its role was to offer a listening service for pupils in the school – a safe forum where pupils could talk freely about interpersonal difficulties and explore possible solutions. If necessary, the peer counsellors could act as advocates for the bullied pupil to tell a member of staff what was happening to them or, preferably, accompany the bullied pupil whilst they themselves told a member of staff. They did not intervene in a bullying situation or tackle the bullying pupils on behalf of another pupil. The major benefits of the service were found to be as follows:

(1) In terms of physical resources the actual service cost little.
(2) A safety net had been created over lunchtimes, especially for

younger pupils and those with special needs. Several set up regular meetings with their chosen peer counsellor and this work focussed on raising self esteem as well as discussing the problems of bullying.

(3) The service gave peer counsellors and receptionists an opportunity to demonstrate responsibility and reliability in a task which had immediate benefits to their school community.

The results of the pilot study were encouraging. The level of usage of the service in the school provided anecdotal evidence that this type of peer support is both needed and valued by staff and pupils. The pupil counsellors, often victims of bullying themselves, gained self-esteem and were able to contribute positively to their school community. They gained skills which will be of benefit to them throughout their lives and appeared to gain a sense of achievement through helping others.

Similar benefits were reported by Konet (1991) who concluded that the entire school can be enriched by the work of a peer support service. In his view the advantages are that: students help students; pupils begin to learn, early in adolescence, how to identify problems and how to work on them; pupils have a say in what affects them; awareness of adolescent issues is heightened; leadership opportunities are offered for the peer counsellors; self-esteem is enhanced in all who participate.

Morey, Miller, Fulton, Rosen and Daley (1989) reported satisfaction by high school students with peer counselling. In their study in one high school, 14 per cent of the pupils used the service, and the majority reported that they would use it again and would recommend it to a friend in need.

Peer counsellors can also be trained as mediators in disputes. (For further reading in the field of conflict resolution see, for example, Leimdorfer, 1992; Kreidler, 1984; Masheder, 1987; Nicholas, 1987; Prutzman, 1978; Walker, 1989.) Their listening skills are helpful in facilitating peaceful conflict resolution by establishing open lines of communication and by making clear ground rules about not allowing name-calling or other 'put-downs'. The peer counsellors are trained to work through four stages in the process:

1. Creating a climate of trust in which parties begin to communicate about the problem.
2. Identifying the problem. This means viewing it from different

perspectives. The peer counsellor (mediator) helps communication by paraphrasing, using open-ended questions and summarising.

3. Exploring alternatives. The peer counsellor generates a list of possible solutions in a non-judgemental way.
4. A plan is made and evaluated. Solutions which are unacceptable are eliminated. Usually it is helpful if the plan is written down.

Peer counselling has the potential to create a context in which pupils can talk through personal issues which concern them or resolve areas of conflict. This can be done through individual counselling or through mediation work. A common theme running through all work on peer counselling and mediation work is the belief that, although personal difficulties and conflicts occur as a normal part of human interaction, both adults and pupils need help in learning how to resolve their difficulties constructively. Where this happens in school settings, interpersonal relationships are enhanced among the pupils and those who abuse their power or status are challenged. The evidence suggests that all involved in the process have learned strategies which will serve them well when they encounter their next area of conflict.

Teachers and power

Teachers are in a very powerful position with respect to their pupils. It may not seem so when faced with a difficult class or a difficult pupil, but the power imbalance between pupils and teachers is indisputable. Not only are teachers adults, but they are also in a situation of having greater knowledge, permission and collective strength than the pupils. This experience of superior power is a part and parcel of what pupils expect from school. Learning how to retain and develop their sense of individuality is part of what children do through school and through their interactions with their teachers. Most teachers for most of the time are sensitive to this, and the way they behave and speak to children reflects it. However, it is all too easy for the tired and harassed teacher inadvertently to belittle or insult a child. Consider, for example, the way in which, as teachers, we talk to children. Visitors to schools often comment if they experience teachers shouting at children – often from quite a distance, such as shouting at a pupil down a corridor, or using pejorative language, or dismissing a pupil's statements or requests. Some pupils will escalate such situations into conflicts, where only the child or young person loses out. The child knows that the teacher – because they are in a position of power as well as being adult – will win in the end. The authors have heard from many parents who are surprised and mystified when their child is admonished for swearing at, or being rude to a teacher when the teacher was rude first!

All young people need effective role models who can demonstrate appropriate behaviours whilst at the same time enjoying a position of power.

Children who are abused at home

This is not a book about child abuse, but we would be negligent not to mention this phenomenon in the context of counselling in education. Children who are abused at home – either physically, emotionally, sexually, or through neglect – have life experiences which are atypical for children. The effects of child abuse are widespread, and there has been much written on this topic.

As we saw in chapter three, work by attachment theorists on clinical populations (Main and Solomon, 1986, 1990) identified a fourth pattern of attachment which they called 'disorganised'. The disorganised child shows no coherent system for dealing with separation and reunion. The reason for this is that the caregiver is at one and the same time the cause of the child's distress and the solution to it. In abusive families, according to one study, 50 per cent of children are anxious-avoidant (Type A), 30 per cent are disorganised (Type D) and only 10 per cent (Type B) are classified as securely attached to their parents (Belsky and Nezworski, 1988). The disorganised child behaves in seemingly inexplicable ways which suggest fear or confusion about the relationship. In older children the disorganised pattern of the relationship with parents emerges in one of two ways. One is related to care-giving. The child may be exceptionally but unnaturally enthusiastic on reunion as if to make sure of pleasing the parent, for fear of what might happen (for example, daughters who have experienced incest showing parent-like behaviours towards their fathers). The other is punitive. The child is directly hostile or ignores the parent. The experience of growing up as an abused child may result, in adulthood, in an expectation that one's child should in turn meet one's emotional or sexual needs, or the adult may be still so preoccupied with meeting the needs of their own parents that they have little energy for caring for their own children.

In adulthood, this pattern is expressed through unresolved mourning over the loss of the attachment figure. It may be that the parent, though present, was experienced by the child as being absent, by not meeting the child's needs, through abuse or violence or neglect. For many survivors of abuse there emerge feelings of guilt, shame and worthlessness which are so strong that they may be repressed out of conscious awareness, even though the events themselves are remembered. This is a small proportion of the population and normally the teacher would not be required to deal with the issues in depth but would refer the child on to another agency. It is still important for educators to know about and to recognise the behaviour patterns.

Children who are not respected as individuals at home are likely either to have difficulty in respecting other adults, or be extremely demanding of time, attention and love as recompense for what they do not receive at home. Teachers would be overstepping their remit in going along with the demands made by an abused child. The teacher cannot be the parent, and cannot offer the love and support which the child needs from her or his parents. The best that the teacher can do is to help the child or young person to come to terms with their situation. So far as counselling is concerned, most children who are the victims of abuse do not want actively to address their abuse, but want to engage in a relationship where they feel safe to discuss other significant factors in their life. The following is a quotation from Sharon, now aged 18, who was sexually abused by her brother from the age of six until nine, and later abused by her foster parent.

> I was sent to a counsellor by my social worker. She said I should talk about what had happened to me, but I didn't want to. The words felt funny and I was worried about what my counsellor wanted me to say. I think she wanted me to cry. In the end I stopped going, and I went to see one of my teachers who had always seemed kind. She let me sit with her for an hour every week instead of going to the library with the rest of the class. I talked to her about all kinds of things. I was very worried about my maths homework at the time and she made me feel okay about it. I think now that what happened was that I had had enough of being treated like an abused child. I just wanted to be Sharon.

CHAPTER EIGHT

Separation, Loss and Grief

Introduction

In this chapter we consider the nature of loss. This could be through bereavement or some other instrument of loss. We will be examining the processes of grieving as they apply in general, and more specifically to children. We will also be looking at the part which adults can play in helping them to cope with the experience of separation from a person whom they love.

As we have seen in earlier chapters, the quality of relationships within the family, and the way in which the family encourages children to view the world and events which occur to them in their lives can enable children to cope with stressful situations. However, no matter how secure and positive children feel in themselves, the experience of loss – through separation, divorce, illness or bereavement – will be disturbing. Loss does not only occur as a function of trauma or death. Other less distressing phenomena can also cause the child to feel grief. For example, the authors have met with many children who have felt grief at leaving one teacher to move to another class – or moving house and leaving friends. In younger children, the loss of a treasured possession can also engender strong feelings. Again therefore we return to the observation, highlighted in chapter one, of other people's feelings and interpretations being personal to them, and the danger of minimising those experiences.

Teachers can play a significant part in supporting children through the various processes of their grieving. With the exception of parents, teachers are often the most significant adult figures in a child's life. This is particularly true in the primary school where the child can expect to remain with one teacher for a year. In the secondary school, where this situation does not pertain, children and young people will frequently adopt a teacher as a trusted role model or confidant.

Responses to loss

If we are to understand how children respond to loss, we must take into consideration a number of factors, including their age; the extent to which they have been prepared for the loss; their relationship with the person whom they have lost, and the way in which the adults close to them are coping with their own grief.

Separation is an unavoidable component in the process of growing up. In fact, the capacity to experience separation anxiety and grief is one of the outcomes of the capacity to love. Children inevitably experience loss in the course of their lives. This may be the death of a pet; the loss of a friend, or, as mentioned earlier, separation from a loved teacher. Each loss which the child or young person experiences needs to be comforted and to be made understandable. In this way the child not only copes with the loss, but also becomes a little more independent.

The caring parent enables the child to keep an appropriate balance between proximity and exploration. This is also true of teacher's relationships with children. Children who have a secure base and who are encouraged to think positively about themselves are more likely to have developed personal qualities which strengthen their capacity to cope. By contrast, insecurely attached children and children with poor self-esteem will have fewer resources to draw on.

Securely attached children are more likely to trust other adults to help them come to terms with, and understand, their own emotional responses to separation and loss. Insecurely attached children are less likely to trust others to understand their feelings. Their response may be to deny what is happening, or to detach themselves from the experience and even appear indifferent to the loss. This can be very difficult for an adult to deal with, as we generally expect certain responses from a bereaved child or adult, and when these do not occur we can be in danger of making assumptions about the strength of feeling based on the paucity of reaction. Each person's experience of, and reactions to separation and loss will be different. There will be wide variation in response, in its intensity and in its duration. Also there will be wide variation in the capacity of bereaved or grieving children to trust or believe in adults' ability to help them.

Bowlby's work proposed a link between the child's experience of loss and later emotional disturbance. He also looked at the role of parents and other caregivers in understanding children's emotional response to separation and in supporting them through the experience. Bowlby's thesis together with studies which have followed on from it have influenced the way in which we now make arrangements for children and separation, in, for example, hospitals.

Because hospitalisation, if it occurs to children, is a necessary condition, it can engender the belief that it is 'for your own good'. This belief makes explanation and comfort redundant. There is now a good deal of evidence of the strength and extent of children's responses to loss of this kind. For example, Robertson and Robertson (1971) were able to demonstrate the profound effects, especially on younger children. They studied children who were in hospital for a short time: they found that the stages which children went through followed a characteristic sequence. First there was **protest**, when the child cried and called out for the parents, and would not be comforted by the staff. Second, there was **withdrawal**, when the children sat listlessly in a state of apparent apathy and indifference. They showed little interest in the staff or in peers. Finally, there was **detachment** when the children seemed to have recovered and become active again. They related to adults and other children, but these relationships appeared shallow, especially if the stay in hospital became prolonged.

When these children were reunited with their parents, typical responses included cold rejection, angry outbursts and excessive clinging. This behaviour could endure for a considerable time after the separation had ended. In fact, if the child stayed in the stage of detachment for too long, it became increasingly difficult to rebond with the attachment figure or to a new caregiver.

The Robertsons' study found that the emotional reactions to separation from parents could be eased if children were given the right sort of support. For example, frequent visits from the parents, being cared for by adults they knew and trusted, being familiarised in advance with the strange environment.

To Bowlby, studies such as this confirmed his view that adults should treat these reactions as natural expressions of separation anxiety. If the child's distress was acknowledged, then it was easier to help the child to deal with it. Where children were discouraged from expressing anger and sadness at the separation or where their emotions were disregarded, there was a much greater likelihood of long-term disturbance. How many post-war babies – now adults – are still suffering from the effects of matter-of-fact hospitalisation or war-time evacuation?

How many Irrational Beliefs are they maintaining as a result of these early separations?

We suggest that the reactions and emotions described by Robertson and Robertson are also sometimes found in children who, as a means towards their own protection, have been removed from their families and placed with foster parents or in children's homes. Children who are accommodated by the local authority (taken into care) tend to suffer separation trauma, and to develop protective mechanisms, often presenting as very friendly and outgoing with strangers, in a superficial way. The trouble starts when they are fostered or adopted, often at a fairly mature age (five years or over.) For example, a brother and sister were placed at ages six and eight with a sympathetic, childless couple in early middle age. They had been abandoned by their mother when the boy was two years old and the girl was a baby. The girl adjusted better to the placement than her brother, but both showed such extreme manipulative and rejecting behaviour in their new home that the fostering broke down. The foster mother, unable to have children of her own, and having given up her teaching job because of her passionate desire to be a mother, managed the children much less well than her husband who was more emotionally detached. There is no easy solution to this problem. Everybody in this scenario had a share in the sadness of loss. The process of bereavement for each was different.

Bowlby's work on bereavement grew out of his studies of separation anxiety. He saw the early reactions of grief following the loss of a loved one as expressing an intense form of separation anxiety. The later stages of grief arose from the realisation that the secure base – the caregivers to whom the child would normally turn for comfort – had gone. These reactions are often enduring and influence adult behaviour.

This is why it is important for teachers to know something about the processes of grieving in order to understand the range and intensity of children's emotional reactions to a loss. It can help the teacher to work appropriately with the child. It can also give clues about whether the child needs more support then the teacher can realistically give.

Divorce and the breakup of relationships

The loss of a parent through divorce or separation is a form of bereavement for the child. One in five children in Britain will have experienced a family break-up by the time they leave school. For many children, this means not only seeing the relationship between father and mother break up, but can also mean that there is a serious break in the relationship with one parent, usually the father. Despite current legislation, there are many cases where the father, either intentionally or through force of circumstance, may lose touch completely with his child or children.

Current debates about the impact of divorce and separation on children highlight controversy. Herbert (1988) suggests that long-term adjustment difficulties are more likely in cases of acrimonious divorce than in cases where a parent has died. In the case of a death, there is a finality through which the child can be supported and comforted. On the other hand, there is no discernible marker for the finality of emotional attachment in the case of divorce.

Some early studies on the effects of divorce and separation on children were badly designed and painted an unnecessarily depressing picture of the outcomes for children of parental separation. Wallerstein et al. (1988) view the issue differently. They see divorce as: 'a process of radically changing family dynamics'. They argue that it is important to look at the family dynamics of parental separation over time and in a social context. Rather than looking at parental separation as a single event, it is more helpful to consider it as part of a longer process which begins with family conflicts and which itself goes through stages. Thus, the nature of the children's reaction varies depending on the child's age and the stage which the separation itself is at.

Some research findings and unsubstantiated perceived wisdom suggest that children from 'broken homes' are more likely to have learning and social problems than children whose families are intact. However, the reality is that there is a wide variation of reactions to divorce due to differences in the factors which facilitate adjustment, such as quality of life; poverty; arrangements for access; the feelings and behaviour of the adults involved; and relationships with the reconstituted family if the parents form new partnerships. Herbert (1988) suggests that children who consider themselves most damaged are: those whose parents were not able to talk to them about the break-up in a reasoned way; those who do not get on well with at least one parent after the break-up; those who are unhappy with the custody arrangements. There is some evidence that boys seem to be more vulnerable than girls in that they are more likely to react strongly at the time and their adjustment can take longer. Some research studies show that girls react more negatively to their mother's remarriage.

It seems, then, that the quality of family relationships is very important, as is the role that the child or young person has within the family and the way they are encouraged to think about themselves. Many effects are noticeable before the parents separate – probably due to conflict and/or arguments and acrimony in the family. This can be a very difficult time for parents who are caught up in their own feelings of distress. Being supportive towards their children can be difficult. Parents often bring their problems to school, when the best thing that the teacher can do is to offer a sympathetic ear and to emphasise the needs of the child at this difficult time. An atmosphere of conflict at the time of separation is more distressing and damaging to the child than the separation itself. Children are also going to be upset if the parent is demonstrably not coping with their own feelings. It is important therefore, not only to listen to the parent but to stress to them the need to communicate to the child about what is happening and to ensure that at least one parent continues to be supportive.

The most difficult situation for children to cope with is when they are used as pawns in the conflicts. They are often the subject of bitter conflict over access and custody. Fortunately, most of these reactions decrease over time, but the extent of their recovery depends greatly on the circumstances and on the support which the child receives. Most children are resilient and, particularly when the situation has been explained to them sensitively and calmly, are able to get on with their lives and to live with and accept their sadness. However, in some cases, the pain of unresolved feelings surrounding separation and loss can resurface in adulthood.

A child who is undergoing a period of grief through loss may well behave in an atypical manner for a while. Teachers can play a key role here in understanding the cause of these behaviours and can help the child to begin to come to terms with the thoughts and feelings surrounding the pain of separation.

Bereavement

The experience of bereavement refers to the responses shown by a person following the loss of a loved one. All societies have developed traditional rituals which accompany a death. These traditions are to honour the dead with little emphasis on the feelings of those left behind. However, these traditions do encompass facilities for mourning. By mourning in a conventional way the individual is given a structure within which to grieve.

Unfortunately, some adults, particularly in Western societies, believe that children are best protected from death and it is rare for children to be given much information on death or on the process of dying. Euphemisms abound such as 'Granny's gone away' or 'Daddy went to sleep and won't wake up'. Also, adults often shield children from the rituals which accompany death and so deny them the opportunity to express their grief.

> We routinely shelter children from death and dying, thinking we are protecting them from harm. But it is clear that we do them a disservice by depriving them of the experience. By making death and dying a taboo subject and keeping children away from people who are dying or who have died, we create fear that need not be there. (Kubler-Ross, 1975, pp. 5–6)

The effects of this can last for a long time. Here, a depressed woman in her thirties recalls what it was like when her mother died.

> When I was seven my mother died after a long illness. My father was so upset by it that he was unable to talk about it and used to shut himself away in his room for hours. Sometimes I saw him hunched up and huddled on the bed. I was sent away to relatives before the funeral and after I came back the matter was never mentioned. All her clothes had gone. There was nothing of her there. It was as if she had never existed. I was not allowed to cry and everyone thought I was all right. But that feeling of emptiness is still with me, just as it was then.

This woman, by her own description, has not come to terms with her own feelings about the death of her mother. One can surmise that she is also still guessing about the nature of her father's feelings. To her, this major life event has not been resolved. She has disregarded her own feelings because she does not know what they are. People in this situation are said to be *unintegrated*. This means that they have not integrated an important part of themselves. The emotional world is disregarded. This can be the adult's reaction to an unresolved childhood trauma.

Grief is a normal, natural and healthy response to bereavement. We all know this, yet are somehow embarrassed by someone else's grief. Adults who have suffered the loss of someone close to them often comment that friends and neighbours withdraw their support after the funeral, as if the work of grieving has now been done. The survivors comment that, in fact, this is when the grief really starts. People withdraw from the griever not from unkindness or disregard but more usually through not realising the course and time involved in the grieving process or because they feel uncomfortable and don't know what to do or how to behave. Sometimes an over-reaction to the survivor can be as unhelpful as continuing support.

As an example, it is useful to look at the case of Simon.

When Simon was 11, his mother died and he was left in the care of his loving step-father. His mother had been ill for some time and Simon was aware of the course of her illness and of her imminent death. In effect, Simon's grieving started before his mother died, and his class teacher was very sympathetic to his situation and wanted to help him as much as possible. Just before his mother's death Simon's behaviour became particularly difficult. He was attention seeking, openly disobedient and defiant. His teacher found this particularly difficult as, because she understood how he must feel, she was prepared for him to be unhappy and to comfort him but not for the challenging behaviours which he displayed. She put up with it and allowed Simon to get away with behaving in a way which she would not accept from anyone else. She found it difficult to be angry with him because he was having such a hard time, and she herself became depressed and very tired, resulting in a long period of time off school. Simon's behaviour continued. In his grief and unhappiness he was challenging the behavioural mores of the school. Through taking advice, Simon's teacher eventually came to realise that by allowing Simon to behave in the way he was, she was not, in fact, helping him, but rather was encouraging habitual bad behaviour.

As caring adults, we are concerned about children who are unhappy. Death does make children unhappy. However, children have the capacity to accept death. It is most important to be able to talk to children in an honest, straightforward way about it. By denying death or by avoiding it the child is not helped to work through the processes of grieving in order to resolve painful feelings.

The process of grieving

By grieving, the person is involved in the psychological and physiological reactions which follow the loss. This grieving does not only relate to death but also to the other losses mentioned earlier. If the bereaved person is not enabled to work through the process of grieving, they may well suffer long-term emotional damage. These symptoms can include: a tendency to dwell on memories of the dead or otherwise absent person; feelings of unreality; anger; moodiness; withdrawal from company.

There are seven stages of the grieving process which have been well established. These do not necessarily occur independently of each other, and may not be identifiable to others. Notwithstanding, the following is the most usual pattern of response to traumatic loss:

1. *Immobilisation.* The individual is likely to feel numbed and overwhelmed. Thoughts and feelings will not be clear. There is now some evidence that children tend not to display this 'psychic numbing', but rather that they tend to the opposite – they are more likely to avoid the situation and become more socially active.
2. *Minimisation.* This is, in effect, a reaction to the feeling of being numbed and frozen. It appears to be a denial of the strength of the feelings. Children may well make comments such as 'There's nothing the matter' or 'What's all the fuss about'. It is difficult for an outsider to experience someone grieving in this way as it falls outside of the crying and depression which we tend to more easily expect.
3. *Depression.* Young children do not tend towards depression in the same way as adults. Simon, in the example above, was demonstrating an alternative to depression. Depression following a loss encompasses feelings of misery, of being helpless and powerless.
4. *Letting go.* This is the stage of accepting reality as it is. A reality which no longer includes a significant other.
5. *Testing.* Here the individual tests out his or her place in this new world. The testing can include testing out new behaviours, new thoughts and sometimes new lifestyles. A friend whose husband died suddenly said that after the funeral she felt that the biggest decision which she had to make was whether or not to redecorate the bedroom. In Simon's case, he was testing out the situation before the death occurred.
6. *Search for meaning.* This search for understanding can be a complicated one. Children may well not have the internal vocabulary to deal with this and could need a good deal of support.
7. *Internalisation.* The new meanings are accepted and acknowledged and the person continues with their life.

This stage model is, we feel, useful in helping those working with bereaved children and adults. It is, however, only a model and should not be interpreted too literally.

Crisis counselling

Post Traumatic Stress Disorder (P.T.S.D.) is a phrase which has been coined to describe the psychological effects over time of having survived a major disaster. There have been many instances of this type over the past few decades such as the Bradford football stadium fire; the sinking of the Zeebrugge ferry; the Hillsborough football disaster. Whilst much has been written about the effects of P.T.S.D. on adults, and therapeutic techniques identified, little has been written about the effects of such trauma on children. Yule and Williams (1992) suggest that adults often deny the effects of such trauma on children. This denial is with the intention of protecting them. However, anybody who has had involvement with children who have suffered such a disaster will know that sometimes the effects manifest themselves not only at home but also at school. The following account from Yule and Williams (1992) describes the behaviour of two pre-school children following the Zeebrugge ferry incident:

> One 4-year-old girl involved her playmates in endless games of nurses patching up the injured, and this went on for many months. A 6-year-old boy drew many pictures of 'the bad ferry' and spoke about it often in class with an understanding teacher. The day that the headteacher took the class, she forbade him talking about it again. That night he began having nightmares and a few months later he tried to kill himself by poking a metal rod into the electric socket. He said he wanted to die to stop the pictures of the bad ferry in his head. (p. 168)

They go on to suggest that as many as 30 to 50 per cent of children will show significant reactions. These could include any or all of the following:

Sleep disturbance: this is fairly common across the ages, particularly in the few weeks following the disaster.
Separation difficulties: some parents found this difficult to cope with, particularly if such clinginess was a regressive form of behaviour which in normal circumstances, the child did not display.
Concentration and memory problems: this was evidenced with old as well as with new materials presented to the child.
Intrusive thoughts: these can occur either with or without an external reminder of the incident.
Talking with parents and peers: children often find this difficult. With parents, children hold back so as not to upset them, and friends often avoid talking about the incident for the same reasons.
Heightened alertness to dangers: this can include a reluctance to engage in situations which had previously been thought of as safe.

Irritability: also, anger, and moodiness.
Guilt: survivors often feel guilty they they have survived when others have died. This has been particularly well documented in the case of adult concentration camp survivors. There has been little written about it in regards to children.
Depression: research following a disaster at sea showed that a small but significant number of children became clinically depressed.
Anxiety and panic: panic reactions are often delayed, and are usually a reaction to some event or incident in the environment.

As can be seen, these reactions are very similar to those of the child grieving over loss of someone close to them.

Teachers in schools where children have been involved in a major disaster become, quite rightly, concerned as to how best to support the children. Usually, not all of the children in a particular class or school have been involved and, with the extensive media coverage which follows disasters teachers are wary of making those children involved a focus of undue interest. The balance between 'carrying on as normal' and meeting the particular needs of the child is a difficult balance. Schools have every right to expect support and advice from outside agencies in determining a consistent approach for the children affected.

Most Local Authorities will have an emergency/disaster plan involving the social services, the medical and the psychological services. Many schools have been instrumental in drawing up such plans for their own community.

Responses to loss at different ages

Very young children can react to loss in a bodily, non-verbal way. They may, for example, become incontinent or suffer loss of appetite. The nature of loss, particularly of a parent through divorce or separation brings it home to children that relationships are not always permanent. Rutter (1975) suggests that the risk of later psychiatric disturbance following the death of a parent is slightly greater if the child is aged three or four and if the parent who dies is the same sex as the child. This could be because the child looses a vital gender role model at a formative stage of development.

Pre-school children often respond by being fearful and sad. They may also show an increase in fearfulness of the dark and at bedtimes. They are likely to be unusually clingy, for example, when being left at playgroup or nursery. They may be unusually aggressive towards their peers or rejecting of adult carers. Fantasies about being abandoned are also quite common.

At the primary school age, children are more able to express sadness and grief about the separation. Sometimes there may be anger directed towards the surviving parent. In the cases of children whose parents have separated, this anger may well be vented on the parent with whom the child is still living. Often this is the mother and she may well be blamed for the separation. It is difficult for the parent in this situation who has to deal with his or her own feelings of loss at the same time as dealing with an angry, hurtful child. It is also common for the absent father to be idealised and for children in this age group to yearn for him.

Pre-adolescent children do not have knowledge of or sensitivity towards the nature of adult relationships. The way in which adults behave is often a mystery – something they take for granted when they feel secure. Whilst they do understand the nature of arguments and of falling out with friends, the nature of the parents relationship is seen as outside of this. Children often find the breakup of the parents' marriage as unbelievable. There is some suggestion that children take on guilt for a separation, and take the blame on themselves. Whilst this is no doubt true in some circumstances, there is little definitive evidence for this suggestion. Everything that we know about children and divorce tells us that the single most important factor is talking to the child.

Pre-adolescent children are more likely to cover up their distress, for example by channelling it into activities. They may be reluctant to share their feelings with other people. This surface lack of concern can give the impression that they do not care, but this impression is likely to mask either anger towards one or both parents or confusion in regards to their own feelings and thoughts.

Teenagers often react to separation or loss of parents by drawing back from the family and concentrating on relationships with the peer group. They may demonstrate anger through disruption or aggression, but this is likely to be short-lived. There is a great need for the teacher to be sensitive and understanding, and to be tolerant of any such changes in behaviour during the period of loss and grieving. However, like Simon's teacher in the example given earlier, the teachers will need to monitor such behaviours over time and to avoid the teenager engaging in habitual unacceptable behaviour. It may be necessary to take advice.

The following are examples and quotations from adults reliving their feelings of grief following separation from a parent, taken from Abrams (1992):

> The only clear indications that I was unhappy – and it was not clear to me at the time – was that I felt sick a lot of the time with a kind of nervous anxiety in my stomach. I didn't like this queasiness, I didn't want to know about it, I certainly didn't want to connect it with my father's death. Instead, I began to overeat. It was easier to feel sick from too much food rather than from grief. (p. 9)

> I can still remember the dragging tiredness which made me long for sleep but wake unrefreshed; the oppressive heaviness that descended with each morning and which sat on my shoulders throughout the day, shifting its weight every now and then in case I forgot even for a moment that it was there. (p. 18)

> Paul was seventeen when his father died of cancer. Years later he still felt guilty that in the final weeks of his father's life he had avoided him, not wanting to touch or be kissed by him . . . (p. 49)

Helping children to grieve

If the teacher is to be helpful to children who are experiencing loss, it is important to be aware of the need for a recognition that the child may be very frightened by what is happening and that this may explain why their behaviour is out of character. Although, as we have seen, there are distinct stages which people typically go through as they grieve, each person responds to loss in a unique way. It is important, therefore, to keep an open, non-judgemental stance towards the child and accept what the child is communicating. It is also important to let the child know that you are not engulfed by the emotions which are being expressed. Too often, when a person attempts to share grief, they are encouraged to stop crying or in others ways to keep a lid on their emotions. This can be extremely unhelpful. The counsellor instead must be prepared to demonstrate empathetic awareness of the strength of feeling in the client yet be strong enough to enter into that person's world in a supportive way. The counsellor must keep that difficult balance between feeling genuine understanding of the pain which the client is suffering and the capacity to stay with these feelings, not be distanced from them. This is where supervision is so helpful to the counsellor since he or she, in turn, can take to supervision any distress which is awakened by being part of another person's grief.

Children, too, need the opportunity to share their grief and to be understood. In families where it is customary to share emotions and be open about them it is usually possible for the child to be supported through the hurt which they experience from loss of whatever kind. Where the families are unable or unused to expressing feelings in this way, it is much more likely that the child will at some point need help.

Particular skill may be needed when counselling children. It is important to be truthful and honest, and not to offer platitudes or euphemisms in a vain attempt to make things better for them. Children are remarkably resilient but it is necessary to be observant in case the child's feelings have simply been buried and not resolved. If children's natural responses – sadness, anger, guilt, fear, helplessness – are repressed by the family, it may be necessary for a teacher/counsellor to adopt a more direct approach than the child's close relatives would do. Playful techniques can be especially effective in overcoming barriers of silence about emotions.

Lendrum and Syme (1992) describe a range of strategies to use in working with children's grief. For example, they encourage the child to draw faces with different expressions on them and then use the faces to identify feelings which are, for example, sad or angry. Similar use can be made of stories, drawing, dance and sounds. Other helpful strategies include making a life-storybook in which the child collects photographs and other mementoes in chronological order of self, family, houses, animals who have died, journeys taken, and so on. Through activities like these, children can be given the opportunity to talk about events and the feelings associated with them.

Lendrum and Syme also point out the importance of enabling the child to say goodbye to the lost person. This may be done face-to-face or symbolically using letters or photographs. If the counsellor gives the child the chance to do this, then much of the work of grieving will have been achieved and the child may then be freed to continue with life and living.

CHAPTER NINE:

Integration of Approaches in Counselling

Introduction

In this book we present a broad overview of key issues for those who are involved in counselling work in schools. We have considered these issues from two distinct perspectives – attachment theory and R.E.T. – which are commonly considered to be radically different from one another.

Attachment theory, as we have seen, is rooted in a psychodynamic model of the person which places great emphasis on unconscious processes and early experiences of relationships. The counsellor working in this tradition will typically interpret much of what clients say or enact in the light of their earlier experiences, whether consciously remembered or not. For this reason, therapeutic use will be made of the actual relationship between the client and the counsellor in the belief that it parallels the client's relationships with significant caregivers in the past. The process of counselling enables the counsellor to reflect back to the client these patterns of relating to others, to bring them into conscious awareness, to deepen the client's understanding of them and to work towards change. Through this change, it is believed, will come new ways of relating to other important figures in the present, including family members, peers and teachers. Counsellors working with children in particular will often use symbolic representations of inner conflicts in order to facilitate the process of change. Poetry, art, sculpting work and play can be very helpful in enabling children and adolescents to externalise their anxieties, fears and anger.

Attachment theory is especially significant for its contribution to our understanding of loss, seen as an essential aspect of human experience. There are many kinds of loss, ranging from common experiences of separation from parents on going to playgroup, starting school, staying away from home right through to traumatic experiences of loss through illness, divorce or bereavement. The way in which the child is supported through feelings engendered by the experience of loss strongly influences emotional patterns which can persist through childhood into adulthood.

The counsellor working within the framework of attachment theory will aim to bring earlier experiences into conscious awareness and work through them in a safe, trusting relationship in order to help the client to make sense of the experience and, where appropriate, to change the internal working model of relationships.

On the other hand, R.E.T. is rooted in the cognitive-behavioural tradition. It places much less emphasis on the past; instead the counsellor working within the R.E.T. framework, will focus more directly on how clients think about themselves and others *in the present*. The counsellor will work with the client to look at Irrational Beliefs, challenge these and so give the client the opportunity to change. In this way, the R.E.T. counsellor uses a structured framework to teach the client new ways of thinking about events and relationships, and thereby helps them to change the emotions which have been created by these thoughts. The starting point will be the exploration of the client's Irrational Beliefs, such as 'I must be liked by all the people in my class.' These beliefs are reflected to the client by the counsellor who will help to dispute them. The client is helped to reframe the Irrational Beliefs by experimenting with alternatives, first within the safety of the counselling room, and later in real-life settings. The emphasis here is less on insight into emotions than on direct action as a means of effecting change.

The two approaches differ most acutely in the following areas:

The developing person

At the heart of attachment theory is knowledge and understanding of human development. This spans experimental research, observational studies and therapeutic casework investigating parent–child relationships, parenting styles, children's patterns of attachment to parents, children's patterns in relating to peers, intergenerational themes, and so on. Attachment theory has made a significant – though at times controversial – contribution to theory and practice in counselling and developmental psychology.

Rational Emotive Therapy by contrast does not dwell on clients' developmental history but focusses on their present set of beliefs about the world, wherever they come from. It does, however, acknowledge that the Irrational Beliefs which we hold now have come about through our interpretation of events in our past. However, overemphasis on the past, from this perspective, can hinder the clients' rational capacity to solve problems as they occur in the present. This clearly is a major difference between the two theories.

Conscious and unconscious processes
As we have seen, the counsellor working in the attachment theory tradition uses the client–counsellor relationship as a means for working through the issues and unresolved conflicts from the past. By taking the role of 'parent-like figure', the counsellor works with the feelings which the client brings to the session and interprets their symbolic meaning. The feelings enacted in the counselling room are the material with which to work out, for example, anger towards authority figures, or feelings of inadequacy in the company of peers.

By contrast, the R.E.T. counsellor takes the role of 'teacher' rather than 'parent' and perceives the relationship as one in which both client and counsellor make a rational appraisal of the problem under consideration. By changing the client's thoughts, the counsellor facilitates change in feelings and behaviour. Again, this is a radical difference between the two approaches. One is concerned to unravel the existential meaning of the person's life while the other focusses on the client's capacity to gain control of his or her life.

The authors of this book came from two different starting-points: Helen Cowie was influenced by the attachment theory perspective, Andrea Pecherek by the stance of R.E.T. Yet despite these differences in theoretical orientation we as authors found that we could work together and share experiences as practitioners without constantly engaging in angry debates. Why was this? It seemed important to explore why we could agree, as practitioners, while our theoretical positions were so different. We decided to examine the common ground.

The nature of the client–counsellor relationship

We found that we both shared, with most counsellors, a commitment to a helping relationship with people suffering emotional distress. We wanted to work with clients to enable them to understand why they felt unhappy, to give them insights into their difficulties (wherever they came from), use strategies from a whole repertoire of skills which we had acquired in our practice to facilitate this process and ultimately to empower our clients to make changes as appropriate for themselves.

We also found that we shared a belief in the client's right to have a positive sense of self. This included enabling clients to look at themselves within their social context and come to understand why and how they came to feel badly about themselves. Closely associated with this belief was a commitment to helping young people in particular to achieve a sense of integration, for example in those aspects of themselves which were in conflict through being highly self-critical or judgemental. We found that we wanted to help our young clients to learn to resolve their own problems and to give them specific techniques which could be useful to them in this task. So it was quite appropriate for each of us to consider teaching our clients new skills in, for example, relating to peers, or challenging injustices such as prejudice and discrimination. Most importantly, perhaps, we each felt that warmth, trust and empathy within the client-counsellor relationship were essential if any therapeutic work was to be done.

The therapeutic lifespan

Practitioners in schools are inevitably bound by constraints of time. We found that, despite differences in theoretical orientation, we were each aware of the effectiveness of short-term therapy which offers a limited number of sessions bound by a clear contract. We each felt the need for counsellors in schools to focus on those clients (the majority of pupils) who would benefit from a small number of sessions, and to be aware of the limits of what they could reasonably offer. We agreed on the need to work intensively with pupils to give them specific skills and strategies for handling difficult situations. We also acknowledged the distinctive knowledge which the teacher/counsellor has of the interactions among groups within the school.

We each felt that group work has an important part to play in making effective use of a counselling approach, as, for example, we showed in the use of the no-blame approach and assertiveness training for dealing with bullying behaviour in schools. Similarly, work on enhancing self-esteem could be done in whole-class settings.

We recommended that there would be times with extremely disturbed pupils when the most helpful strategy would be to refer the client on to a counsellor outside the school setting who could offer in-depth counselling over a longer period of time. No matter how successful schools are in dealing with the issues which we have discussed in this book, there will remain a residue of seriously disturbed individuals who will require counselling in a setting away from the school. Given these constraints, however, we found that we each shared a concern to establish trust in the relationship with the client, to focus on the issue, to work intensively on that issue, and to prepare the client for the termination of counselling.

Working towards change

Attachment theorists have developed (and continue to develop) the concept of the internal working model of relationships. This offers a framework to counsellors for effecting change in their clients in a very practical way which has strong parallels with the R.E.T. counsellor's concept of the client's 'set of beliefs about the world' or 'basic assumptions'.

From each perspective, the counsellor works with the client's beliefs, often long-held and resistant to change, in order to create new representations with which to make predictions about people and to form new relationships. The child who has had stable, secure experiences is likely to have a world-view which is benign and in which the self is worthy of love. But children who have had negative experiences are much more likely to view the world and the people in it as threatening, and themselves as unlovable. We agreed that it is these latter 'faulty' models which we as counsellors need to change, since the strategies which the child has evolved to protect the self from harm will most certainly limit and hinder the capacity to relate effectively to others, and to feel positively about themselves. From both perspectives – attachment theory and R.E.T. – we found that the counsellor views defensive strategies as in need of change and will work constructively with the client to effect this change.

Loss

We each found that in our work it had been necessary to consider the issue of loss when dealing with young people. Of course our emphasis varied but, despite our differences, we had each found the need to take into account the emotional distress experienced by children through loss and, in particular, by the failure to be allowed to grieve. We also shared a belief in giving children and young people the opportunity to express their feelings of sadness, anger and hate within the counselling relationship and to understand that these feelings come from somewhere and that there is a reason for them. We each agreed about the need for counsellors to acknowledge this kind of pain through empathic understanding, but, having done that to move on to practical action for change. We showed how this could be achieved, for example, through family sculpt work as a means of enabling children to explore feelings of loss, either individually or in the safety of a group.

Integration or eclecticism?

We recommend to counsellors in educational settings that they feel comfortable with their own model of counselling but that, at the same time, they retain a healthy curiosity about the ways in which other counsellors work. This could be interpreted to mean a tolerance of alternative viewpoints and a form of eclecticism with regard to practical strategies for action.

Some counsellors, of course, campaign actively against eclecticism and argue a strong case for distinctiveness in theoretical approaches to therapeutic work with clients. However, after our experience of working together, we came to the conclusion that it was possible to maintain a commitment to a particular theoretical perspective while at the same time being open to different ideas and techniques to suit the particular needs of the client. We felt that this openness was not superficial. Instead, we each felt that we were engaged in a process of personal integration of ideas rather than a rigid adherence to one orthodoxy. Perhaps in each case this illustrated awareness of the limitations of any one stance and a willingness to develop a model in the light of changing ideas.

Clearly this was possible at a practical level, and, in fact, is common in our discipline. Most counsellors are eager to broaden their areas of expertise and, because of the immediacy of their work, are more than ready to apply different techniques and observe their outcomes in a pragmatic way. But for us it seemed to mean more than this. The writing of the book became part of a personal process of development through which each of us felt enhanced: Helen Cowie found the R.E.T. strategies to be liberating for the empowerment of children experiencing the abuse of power; Andrea Pecherek found herself drawing more extensively on the attachment theory literature for her work on bereavement counselling with pupils, and in preparing guidelines for teachers to deal with crisis counselling following disasters.

We found in our dialogues with one another that our friendship grew, and that we could more freely offer each other insights into work with clients. The professional integrated with the personal through a deepening respect for each other's viewpoint. We were able to acknowledge differences and yet to work with them. Finally, we were no longer constrained by the need to agree on every point but to appreciate diversity in the complex field of counselling. You could do the same.

References

Abrams, R. (1992) *When Parents Die* (London: Charles Lett).

Adelman, C. (1989) 'Overview' in C. Harber and R. Meighan, *The Democratic School* (Ticknall: Education Now Books).

Ainsworth, M., Blehar, M. C., Waters, E. and Wall, S. (1978) *Patterns of attachment: A Psychological Study of the Strange Situation* (Hillsdale, N.J.: Lawrence Erlbaum Associates).

Anthony, B. D. (1982) 'Lesbian client – lesbian therapist: opportunities and challenges in working together', *Journal of Homosexuality,* **7**, 45–57.

Arora, T. (1989) 'Bullying – action and intervention', *Pastoral Care in Education,* **7**, 44–47.

Arora, T. (1991) 'The use of victim support groups' in P. K. Smith and D. Thompson (eds.) *Practical Approaches to Bullying* (London: David Fulton).

B.A.C. (1984) *Code of Ethics and Practice for Counsellors* (Rugby: British Association for Counselling).

Belsky, J. and Nezworski, T. (1988) *Clinical Implications of Attachment* (Hillsdale, N.J.: Erlbaum).

Best, R. E. (1989) 'Pastoral care: Some reflections and a Re-statement' in *Pastoral care in Education,* **7**(4), 7–13.

Blackburn, I. M. (1986) 'The cognitive revolution: an ongoing evolution', *Behavioural Psychotherapy,* **14**(4), 274–7.

Blom, C. E., Cheny, B. D. and Snoddy, J. E. (1986) *Stress in Childhood: An intervention model for teachers and other professionals* (New York: Teachers College Press).

Bowlby, J. (1958) 'The nature of the child's tie to his mother', *International Journal of Psychoanalysis,* **39**, 350–73.

Bowlby, J. (1969) *Attachment and Loss: Attachment* (New York: Basic Books).

Bowlby, J. (1973) *Attachment and Loss: Separation* (New York: Basic Books).

Bowlby, J. (1980) *Attachment and Loss: Loss, Sadness and Depression* (New York: Basic Books).

Carey, P. (1993) 'Dealing with pupils' life crises: A model for Action', *Pastoral Care in Education,* **11**(3), 12–18.

Carr, R. (1981) *Theory and Practice of Peer Counselling* (Ottawa: Canada Employment and Immigration).

Carr, R. (1988) 'The City-wide peer counselling program', *Children and Youth Services Review,* **10,** 217–32.

Clemett, A. J. Pearce, J. S. (1986) *The Evaluation of Pastoral Care* (Oxford: Blackwell).

Coopersmith, S. (1967) *The Antecedents of Self-esteem* (San Francisco: Freeman).

Corby, B. (1993) *Child Abuse: Towards a knowledge base* (Buckingham: Open University Press).

Cowie, H. and Rudduck, J. (1988) *Learning Together, Working Together* (London: BP Educational Services).

Cowie, H. and Rudduck, J. (1990) *Cooperative Learning: Traditions and Transitions* (London: BP Educational Service).

Cowie, H., Sharp, S. and Smith, P. K. (1992) 'Tackling bullying in schools: the method of common concern', *Education Section Review,* **16**(2), 55–7.

Cowie, H., Smith, P. K., Boulton, M. and Laver, R. (1994) *Cooperation in the Multi-ethnic Classroom* (London: David Fulton).

Davie, R. (1993) 'Listen to the child: a time for change', *The Psychologist,* **6**(6), 252–57.

De Francis, V. (1969) *Protecting the child victim of sex crimes committed by adults* (Denver: American Humane Association).

DES (1989) *Discipline in Schools. Report of the Committee of Enquiry Chaired by Lord Elton* (London: HMSO).

DfE (1992) *Choice and Diversity: a New Framework for Schools* (London: HMSO).

Doherty, W. J. (1993) 'I'm OK, you're OK, but what about the kids?', *Family Therapy Networker,* Sept., 53.

Dorner, D. (1989) *Die Logik des Misslingens* (Reinbek: Rowohlt).

Dryden, W. (1990) *Rational Emotive Counselling in Action* (London: Sage Publications).

Dryden, W. (1991) *A Dialogue with John Norcross* (Milton Keynes: Open University Press).

Egan, M. (1986) *The Skilled Helper* (Pacific Grove, C.A.: Brooks/Cole).

Eggleston, J. (1985) *The Educational and Vocational Experiences of 15–18-year-old Young People of Minority Ethnic Groups* (University of Keele: Department of Education).

Ellis, A. (1984) 'The essence of RET – 1984' *Journal of Rational Emotive Therapy,* **2**(1), 19–25.

Gersch, I. (1992) 'Pupil involvement in assessment' in T. Cline (ed.) *Assessment of Special Educational Needs: International Perspectives* (London: Routledge).

Gomes-Schwartz, B., Horowitz, J. and Cardarelli, A. (1990) *Child sexual abuse: The initial effects* (Beverley Hills, C.A.: Sage).

Gurney, P. W. (1986) 'Self-esteem in the classroom', *School Psychology International,* **1**(4), 86.

Hamblin, D. (1978) *The teacher and pastoral care* (Oxford: Blackwell).

Harter, S. (1985) 'Competence as a dimension of self-evaluation: towards a comprehensive model of self-worth', in R. L. Leahy (ed.) *The Development of the Self* (Orlando, Fl.: Academic Press).

Hartley, R. L. (1986) 'Imagine you're clever' *Journal of Child Psychology and Psychiatry,* **11**(3), 175.

Herbert, M. (1988) *Working with Children and their Families* (Leicester: BPS Books).

Hobbs, N. (1975) *The Future of Children* (San Francisco, C.A.: Jossey-Bass).

Holmes, J. (1993) *John Bowlby and Attachment Theory* (London: Routledge).

Hopson, B. and Scally, M. (1981) *Lifeskills Teaching* (London: McGraw Hill).

James, W. (1961) *Psychology: the Briefer Course* (New York: Harper Row).

Karasu, T. B. (1986) 'The specificity versus nonspecificity dilemma: toward identifying therapeutic change agents', *American Journal of Psychiatry*, 687–95.

Kaser, R. (1993) 'A change in focus ... without losing sight of the child: an ecological-systems approach', *School Psychology International*, **14**(1), 5–19.

Kelly, G. (1955) *The Psychology of Personal Constructs* (New York: Norton).

Kitzinger, C. (1987) *The Social Construction of Lesbianism* (London: Sage).

Konet, R. (1991) 'Peer helpers in the middle school', *Middle School Journal*, Sept., 13–15.

Kreidler, W. (1984) *Creative Conflict Resolution* (Glenview Ill.: Scott, Foresman and Compa).

Kubler-Ross, E. (1975) *Death: the Final Stage of Growth* (New York: Simon and Schuster).

Lang, P. (1983) 'How pupils see it' in *Pastoral Care in Education* **1**(3), 164–74.

Lang, P. and Ribbins, P. (1985) 'Pastoral Care', in T. Husen and T. Postlethwaite (eds.) *International Encyclopaedia of Education* (London: Pergamon).

Lawrence, G. (1973) *Improved reading through counselling* (Ward Lock: London).

Leimdorfer, T. (1992) *Once Upon a Conflict* (London: Education Advisory Committee).

Lendrum, S. and Syme, G. (1992) *Gift of Tears* (London: Routledge).

London, P. (1987) 'Character Education and clinical intervention: A Paradigm shift for US schools', *Phi Delta Kappan*, May, 667–73.

Main, M. and Solomon, J. (1986) 'Discovery of an insecure/disorganised attachment pattern' in T. B. Brazelton and M. W. Yogman (eds.) *Affective Development in Infancy* (Norwood, N.J.: Ablex).

Main, M. and Solomon, J. (1990) 'Procedures for identifying infants as disorganised/disoriented during the Ainsworth Strange Situation' in M. T. Greenwood, D. Cicchetti and E. M. Cummings (eds.) *Attachment in the Preschool Years* (Chicago, Ill.: University of Chicago Press).

Maines, B. and Robinson, G. (1991) 'Don't beat the bullies!' *Educational Psychology in Practice*, **7**(3), 168–72.

Maines, B. and Robinson, G. (1992) *Michael's story: the 'no-blame approach'* (Bristol: Lame Duck Publications).

Masheder, M. (1987) *Let's Cooperate* (London: Peace Pledge Union).

Maxime', J. (1991) *Black Identity: Workbook One of Black Like Me Series* (2nd edition). London: Emani Publications.

Maxime', J. (1993) 'The therapeutic importance of racial identity in working with black children who hate', in V. Varma (ed.) *How and Why Children Hate* (London: Jessica Kingsley).

Morey, R., Miller, D., Fulton, R., Rosen, L. and Daley, J. (1989) *School Counsellor*, **37**, 137–43.

Mosley, J. (1993a) *Turn Your School Round* (Wisbech: Learning Development Aids).

Mosley, J. (1993b) 'A whole-school approach to self-esteem and positive behaviour', *Topic,* **4**(9), 1–4.

Murgatroyd, S. (1985) *Counselling and Helping* (London: BPS and Routledge).

Newall, P. (1993) 'Too young to be kept in chains', *Times Educational Supplement,* p. 27.

Nicholas, F. M. (1987) *Coping with Conflict: a Resource Book for the Middle Years.* London: Learning Development Aids.

O'Connor, P. (1992) *Friendships Between Women* (London: The Guilford Press).

Pikas, A. (1989) 'A pure concept of mobbing gives the best results for treatment', *School Psychology International,* **10,** 95–104. A similar article appears in E. Roland and E. Munthe (eds.) *Bullying: an International Perspective* (London: David Fulton).

Plas, J. M. (1986) *Systems Psychology in the Schools* (New York: Pergamon).

Poppleton, P., Deas, R., Gray, J., Harrison, B., Lindsay, G., Sharples, H. and Thompson, D. (1985) *Aspects of Care in Schools* (Sheffield: University of Sheffield, Department of Education Papers in Education).

Prutzman, P. (1978) *The Friendly Classroom for a Small Planet* (New Jersey: Avery).

Robertson, J. and Robertson, J. (1971) 'Young children in brief separation', in R. K. Eissler et al. (eds.) *The Psychoanalytic Study of the Child,* **26** (New Haven, Conn.: Yale University Press).

Robinson and Maines, B. (1988) 'They can because . . .' *A workshop in print.* (Maidstone: Redhill School).

Rogers, C. R. (1951) *Client-centered Therapy* (Boston: Houghton Mifflin).

Rogers, C. R. (1967) *The Therapeutic Relationship and its Impact* (Madison: University of Wisconsin Press).

Rutter, M. (1975) *Helping troubled children* (Harmondsworth: Penguin).

Salmon, P. and Claire, H. (1984) *Classroom Collaboration* (London: Routledge).

Saltzman, N. and Norcross, J. (1990) (eds.) *Therapy Wars: Contention and Convergence in Differing Clinical Approaches* (San Francisco: Jossey-Bass).

Sharp, S., Sellars, A. and Cowie, H. (1994) 'Time to listen: setting up a peer counselling service to help tackle the problem of bullying in school', *Pastoral Care in Education.*

Sharp, S. and Smith, P. K. (eds.) (1994) *Tackling Bullying in Your School* (London: Routledge).

Sharp, S. and Smith, P. K. (1991) 'Bullying in school: the DfE Sheffield Bullying Project', *Early Child Development and Care,* **77**, 47–55.

Sharp, S. and Thompson, D. (1992) 'Sources of Stress: A contrast between pupil perspective and pastoral teachers' perceptions', *School Psychology International,* **13**(3), 229–42.

Silveira, W. R. and Trafford, G. (1988) *Children Need Groups* (Aberdeen: Aberdeen University Press).

Sinanson, V. (1993) *Mental handicap and the human condition: New approaches from the Tavistock* (London: Free Association Press).

Smith, P. K., Bowers, L., Binney, V. and Cowie, H. (1993) 'Relationships of children involved in bully-victim problems at school', in S. Duck (ed.) *Learning about Relationships* (London: Sage).

Smith, P. K. and Sharp, S. (1994) *School Bullying: Insights and Perspectives* (London: Routledge).

Speltz, M. (1990) 'The treatment of pre-school conduct problems: an integration of behavioural and attachment concepts' in M. T. Greenberg, D. Cicchetti and M. Cumins (eds.) *Attachment in the Pre-school Years: theory, research and intervention* (Chicago: Chicago University Press).

Stern, D. (1985) *The Interpersonal World of the Infant* (New York: Basic Books).

Swann Report (1985) *Education for All* (London: HMSO).

Troy, M. and Sroufe, L. A. (1987) 'Victimization among preschoolers: role of attachment relationship history', *Journal of the American Academy of Child and Adolescent Psychiatry,* **26,** 166–72.

Troyna, B. and Hatcher, R. (1992) *Racism in Children's Lives* (London: Routledge).

Turner, P. (1991) 'Relations between attachment, gender, and behavior with peers in preschool', *Child Development,* **62,** 1475–88.

Van Ijzendoorn, M. and Kroonenberg, P. (1988) 'Cross-cultural patterns of attachment: a meta-analysis of the Strange Situation', *Child Development,* **59,** 147–56.

Walen, S. R., DiGuiseppe, R. and Wessler, R. L. (1980) *A Practitioner's guide to Rational-Emotive Therapy* (New York: Oxford University Press).

Walker, J. (1989) *Violence and Conflict Resolution in Schools* (Brussels: Quaker Council for European Affairs).

Wallerstein, J. S., Corbin, S. B. and Lewis, J. M. (1988) 'Children of divorce: a 10-year study' in E. M. Hetherington and J. D. Arasteh (eds.) *Impact of Divorce, Single Parenting and Stepparenting on Children* (Hillsdale, N.J.: Erlbaum).

Wedge, P. and Essen, J. (1982) *Children in Adversity* (London: Pan Books).

Whitney, I. and Smith, P. K. (1993) 'A survey of the nature and extent of bullying in junior/middle and secondary school', *Educational Research,* **35**(1), 3–25.

Wright, C. (1992) *Race Relations in the Primary School* (London: David Fulton).

Yule, W., and Williams, R. M. (1992) 'The Management of trauma following disasters' in *Child and Adolescent Therapy – a handbook* D. A. Lane and A. Miller (ed.) (Milton Keyenes: Open University Press).

Index

Author Index

Subject Index